Shine Your Eyes: Ch ***rry***

ISBN: 978-1-60188-017-8

FIRST EDITION

Published by Olatokunbo Ojo
For more information and book orders:
Call: +44 07760967528
Email address: ttaservices2021@gmail.com

Edited by Productivity Insights Limited

Table of Contents

Introduction

This book serves as a spiritual guide for individuals seeking meaningful relationships. It aims to illuminate the journey of finding a life partner through the lens of faith, emphasising how God can lead us to our true match.

I am writing this book to all singles to shine their eyes and not make any mistakes by marrying for the wrong reason.

When marriage fails, it is because they choose the wrong person, this does not necessarily mean the person has a bad character, but your values and beliefs are misaligned. This is a foundational factor that many ignore during courtship. I wrote this book Shine Your Eyes because people sometimes enter marriage for reasons that may not be sustainable or healthy. These choices often stem from emotional, social, or psychological motivations. Here are some of the most common wrong reasons why people get married:

1. Social Pressure:

Many people feel pressured by family, friends, or society to get married, especially at a certain age. This pressure can lead them to settle for a partner they may not be compatible with, prioritising timing over a meaningful connection.

2. Fear of Loneliness:

The fear of loneliness can lead people to marry someone they neither love nor are truly compatible with. They may feel that a flawed relationship is better than no relationship, hoping that companionship will fill the void.

3. Escaping a Situation:

Some individuals marry to escape a difficult situation, like a challenging family environment or financial struggles. However, marriage contracted under this stress can lead to new and equally challenging issues if compatibility isn't strong.

4. Financial or Economic Stability:

While financial stability is an understandable consideration, marrying solely for financial security or material gain often results in dissatisfaction without a deeper, genuine connection. Financial issues can also shift over time, adding stress to a relationship.

5. Physical Attraction or Infatuation:

Early-stage infatuation or intense physical attraction can cloud judgment, leading people to marry without truly understanding their partner's character or values. As these feelings wane over time, the reality of incompatibility may become more evident.

6. Rebound from a Previous Relationship:

After a breakup, some people rush into marriage with someone new, seeking comfort and validation. This "rebound" relationship often doesn't have the foundation of a stable, self-aware choice, making long-term satisfaction less likely.

7. Unresolved Personal Issues:

People dealing with low self-esteem, anxiety, or insecurity may seek marriage to feel validated or secure. However, unresolved personal issues can make it challenging to maintain a balanced, healthy relationship and often place undue pressure on the marriage.

8. Parental or Cultural Expectations:

In many cultures, marriage is seen as an expected life step, and some people feel obligated to marry a specific type of partner or by a certain age due to cultural norms. These marriages may lack a genuine personal connection, as they are driven more by duty than desire.

9. Wanting to Meet Milestones:

Some individuals marry because they feel it's "time" to meet social milestones (marriage, kids, etc.), even if they're not with the right person. This sense of urgency can lead to compromise on compatibility or love.

10. Desire to Change or 'Fix' the Partner:

Marrying with the hope that a partner will change in certain ways often backfires. People sometimes believe that marriage will "fix" traits they don't like, but marriage is unlikely to change a person's core personality, values, or habits.

11. Pregnancy:

When faced with an unexpected pregnancy, some couples feel compelled to marry. While some such marriages succeed, they can be strained if they were only initiated due to the pregnancy and not mutual desire and compatibility.

12. Seeking Social Validation or Status:

In some cases, people marry to attain a certain social status or to gain admiration from others. This can happen in social circles or cultures where marriage is highly prised, leading people to prioritise appearance over actual relationship health.

13. Romanticised or Idealised Notions of Marriage:

Many have idealistic expectations of marriage from movies, books, or societal portrayals. They may marry under the misconception that marriage will lead to happiness, overlooking the hard work and compatibility required to sustain it.

14. Pressure to Start a Family:

Some individuals, especially those who want children, feel a strong urge to marry quickly to meet biological timelines or family expectations, sometimes compromising compatibility in the rush to have children.

Understanding these factors can help people reflect on their true motivations and hopefully make more thoughtful, long-lasting choices when considering marriage. Also, people do not have a full understanding of what marriage is all about.

Marriage is more than physical attributes. When the decision to marry is premised solely on physical attraction, it is unable to hold and then couples divorce. This leads to negative narratives about marriage. The truth is that marriage is good if you choose the right partner, which is what the book is all about. It was written so that you can select the right partner to marry as God desired it to be. Also, its purpose is to change wrong perspectives about marriage. Marriage is good because God created it, and everything that God created is good. The problem is not marriage, but the person you choose to spend the rest of your life with. This book will point out what you should look out for before you say, "I do," and the different wrong reasons why people get married, which should be avoided. A marriage without God at the centre will be disastrous.

I hope as you read this book it will transform you and prepare you to shine your eyes when choosing your life partner. Remember, marriage is meant to last for a lifetime.

Proper preparation + The right choice = A Blissful marriage.

There is no perfect marriage because it is two people from different backgrounds, values, and beliefs coming together to be one.

Anonymous Testimony: Her Journey to Finding the Right Partner

The journey to finding a life partner was neither straight nor simple. It was filled with moments of joy, deep heartache, confusion, and ultimately, profound spiritual growth. For much of her early adulthood, she was focused on finding "the one," but her focus was misplaced. It was only when she fully surrendered her desires to God and placed her trust in His timing that she found the partner He had prepared for her.

Her Struggles: Trusting in Her Timing

In her early 20s, she believed she had a clear idea of what she wanted in a partner. She envisioned someone who shared her interests, could make her laugh, and who, on the surface, seemed like the perfect match. She had long prayed for God to bring someone into her life, but her impatience often led her to take matters into her own hands. She found herself entering relationships hastily, mistaking fleeting attraction for lasting love.

One relationship seemed promising at first. They met at church, bonded over their shared faith, and quickly became inseparable. On the outside, everything looked perfect, but internally, she felt a subtle unrest. She often ignored those feelings, convincing herself that no relationship is flawless. As time went on, however, it became clear that while they shared a surface-level connection, their core values and long-term goals didn't align. He wanted a lifestyle of stability and comfort, while she felt called to more adventurous service in ministry, even if it meant sacrifices.

There were other differences, too — communication styles, priorities, and ultimately, their commitment to growing together spiritually.

After nearly two years of trying to make it work, the relationship ended. She was heartbroken and confused. She had prayed, and yet, it felt like God had let her down. Why had this relationship failed when it started with such promise? Disappointed, she questioned whether she could trust God with her heart.

Lessons Learned: The Importance of Surrender and Healing

Looking back, she realised that this season of heartbreak was crucial to her growth. After the breakup, she went through a long period of self-reflection. She had to face the fact that she had been trying to fit people into God's plan for her life rather than allowing God to reveal His plan for her relationships. She also recognised that she had been seeking fulfillment in a partner rather than God.

During this time, she intentionally took a break from dating to focus on her relationship with God. She immersed herself in scripture, prayed more, and sought wise counsel from mentors and friends. Psalm 37:4 became her guiding verse: "Delight yourself in the Lord, and He will give you the desires of your heart." She realised that delighting in God meant surrendering her desires and trusting Him to shape them according to His will.

One of the most powerful lessons she learned during this time was the importance of healing. She had to let go of the hurt, disappointment, and unrealistic expectations she had placed on her past relationships. She spent time journaling, praying for healing, and asking God to prepare her heart for the right person — whenever that might be.

The Pivotal Role of Faith: God's Timing, Not Mine

As she deepened her relationship with God, her perspective on relationships shifted. She stopped viewing singleness as a burden and instead saw it as a season of preparation. She trusted that if God had someone for her, it would happen in His time, not hers.

Months passed, and while she occasionally wondered when God's plan would unfold, she found peace while waiting. It was during this time that she met someone new – someone who, at first glance, seemed different from the "ideal" she had once envisioned. They met through a mutual friend in ministry, and their connection grew slowly. Unlike previous relationships, this one wasn't marked by intense emotional highs or dramatic sparks. Instead, it was characterised by peace, mutual respect, and a shared commitment to growing in faith together.

What stood out most was how they both prioritised God in their lives. They prayed together from the start, something she had never done consistently in her past relationships. Their conversations were honest and intentional, and they both sought God's will, not just their desires. As their relationship deepened, she began to understand what it meant to be equally yoked – not just in shared beliefs, but in their vision for the future, their values, and their mission to serve others.

The Right Relationship: A Union Rooted in Faith

As she continued to seek God's guidance, she realised that this relationship felt different. It wasn't about chasing an ideal or fulfilling a checklist – it was about building something that honoured God. Over time, she saw how this person embodied many of the qualities she had prayed for: integrity, kindness, emotional maturity, and a deep commitment to Christ.

Faith played a pivotal role in every step of their relationship. They didn't rush; instead, they took time to seek God's will, and they actively involved their community in their journey. They sought advice from mentors, prayed for clarity, and prioritised spiritual growth over surface-level compatibility.

Eventually, she knew that this was the partner God had prepared for her. It wasn't a relationship that she had orchestrated through her efforts or impatience – it was one that God had brought into her life when she was ready to receive it. When they got married, it wasn't just the fulfillment of a personal dream, but the beginning of a union that they both believed would glorify God and serve others.

Trusting God with Your Heart

Her journey to finding the right partner was marked by struggles, but each struggle brought growth. She learned to surrender her desires, trust God's timing, and prioritise her relationship with Him over everything else. When she stopped trying to force relationships to fit her timeline and trusted God with her heart, He blessed her with a partner who exceeded her expectations in the most important ways – someone who helps her grow closer to God, challenges her to live out her faith, and walks alongside her in service to others.

For anyone seeking a partner, her greatest advice is to trust in God's perfect plan. He knows your heart, your desires, and your needs better than you do. Surrender your journey to Him, focus on becoming the person He's called you to be, and in His time, He will bring the right person into your life. Faith isn't just a part of the process – it's the foundation on which lasting, God-honouring relationships are built

- By Anonymous

1

Understanding God's Design For Relationships

In this chapter, we start by exploring the biblical foundations of marriage and relationships, emphasising that God's design is intentional. From the beginning of creation, God designed man and woman to complement each other and serve a greater purpose (Genesis 2:18-24). Marriage is seen as a covenant, not just between two individuals, but between the couple and God, which means that relationships are meant to reflect God's love and purpose.

The chapter explains how the union of a man and a woman should glorify God, serve others, and allow the couple to grow together in their faith. Choosing a partner is more than fulfilling personal desires; it's about partnering with someone who shares your faith and purpose and supports you in your walk with God and the purpose for which you were created.

God's Intentions for Marriage: A Biblical Foundation

Marriage is one of the most significant and sacred institutions in the Christian faith. From the beginning, the Bible clearly defines what God intends marriage to be. It is more than just a personal or social contract between two people; it is a covenant relationship designed by God to reflect His love, faithfulness, and purpose. Through marriage, God illustrates spiritual truths about His relationship with humanity, and He intends for married couples to fulfil a greater purpose in His plan for creation.

By examining key scriptures, we can better understand God's intentions for marriage and its higher purpose in His kingdom.

The Creation of Marriage - Genesis 2:18-24

The first mention of marriage appears in the creation story in Genesis, where God establishes the union between Adam and Eve, laying the foundation for what marriage is meant to be:

> *The Lord God said, 'It is not good for the man to be alone. I will make a helper suitable for him. '*
>
> *Genesis 2:18 (NIV)*

Here, God acknowledges Adam's need for companionship, indicating that human beings are created for relationships.

God creates Eve, the first woman, from Adam's rib, signifying their unique bond:

> *"So the Lord God caused the man to fall into a deep sleep; and while he was sleeping, He took one of the man's ribs and then closed up the place with flesh. Then the Lord God made a woman from the rib He had taken out of the man, and He brought her to the man."*
>
> *Genesis 2:21-22 (NIV)*

Adam's response highlights the depth of connection and unity between man and woman:

> *"This is now bone of my bones and flesh of my flesh; she shall be called 'woman,' for she was taken out of man. For this reason, a man will leave his father and mother and be united to his wife, and they will become one flesh."*
>
> *Genesis 2:23-24 (NIV)*

Key Points

- ***Companionship and Partnership***: God's first intention for marriage is to provide companionship. "It is not good for man to be alone," speaks to the inherent need for relationships that support, love, and nurture.

- ***Unity and Oneness:*** Marriage is intended to be a union where two individuals become "one flesh." This not only refers to physical unity but also emotional, spiritual, and relational oneness.
- ***Equality and Complementarity***: While man and woman are distinct, they are equal in value and purpose. The woman is created as a "helper suitable" for the man, meaning that both.

Marriage as a Reflection of Christ and the Church - Ephesians 5:25-33

In the New Testament, the Apostle Paul provides one of the most profound insights into the purpose of marriage in his letter to the Ephesians. In this passage, Paul likens the relationship between a husband and wife to the relationship between Christ and His Church:

> *"Husbands, love your wives, just as Christ loved the church and gave Himself up for her to make her holy,*

> *cleansing her by the washing with water through the word, and to present her to Himself as a radiant church, without stain or wrinkle or any other blemish, but holy and blameless."*
>
> *Ephesians 5:25-27 (NIV)*

This instruction to husbands highlights the sacrificial love that Christ demonstrated for the Church. In the same way, husbands are called to love their wives selflessly, putting their needs and well-being first, just as Christ sacrificed Himself for the sake of humanity.

Paul continues by affirming the oneness of marriage, drawing on the Genesis account:

> *"For this reason, a man will leave his father and mother and be united to his wife, and the two will become one flesh."*
>
> *Ephesians 5:31 (NIV)*

Paul concludes by stating that marriage is a profound mystery that reveals something greater than itself:

"This is a profound mystery—but I am talking about Christ and the church."

Ephesians 5:32 (NIV)

Key Points

- ***Sacrificial Love*:** Husbands are called to love their wives as Christ loved the Church—selflessly, sacrificially, and unconditionally. This sets the highest standard for love within marriage.
- ***Spiritual Leadership and Care*:** The husband's role is not to dominate but to nurture his wife's spiritual growth, helping her to grow in holiness and righteousness, just as Christ leads the Church.
- ***Mutual Submission*:** Paul also calls for mutual submission (Ephesians 5:21), meaning that both husband and wife should submit to one another out of reverence for Christ. This implies respect, love, and service to one another.
- ***Marriage Reflects Christ's Love:*** Marriage is designed to be a living picture of Christ's love for the Church. Just as Christ is committed to His bride, the Church, husbands,

and wives are called to reflect that same commitment and love in their marriages.

The Higher Purpose of Marriage: Fulfilling God's Plan

Marriage in the Bible is never just about the individuals involved; it always serves a greater purpose. God designed marriage to reflect His relationship with humanity, to fulfil His purposes on earth, and to contribute to society's flourishing.

More of God's purposes for marriage include:

Reflecting God's Character and Love

Marriage reflects God's covenantal love and faithfulness. In the same way that God enters a covenant relationship with His people, marriage is a covenant where both partners commit to love, honour, and cherish one another for life. This mirrors the unbreakable bond that God has with His people. But at the beginning of creation God 'made them male and female.'

> *'For this reason a man will leave his father and mother and be united to his wife, and the two will become one flesh.' So they are no longer two, but one flesh. Therefore what God has joined together, let no one separate."*
>
> *Mark 10:6-9 (NIV)*

Fulfilling God's Purpose for Creation

In Genesis 1:28, God commands Adam and Eve to "be fruitful and multiply and fill the earth and subdue it." Marriage is part of God's plan for procreation and stewardship of the earth. Through marriage, families are formed, and these families become the building blocks of society. Christian marriages are also meant to raise the next generation to know and follow God, fulfilling the Great Commission (Matthew 28:19-20) by making disciples.

Marriage as a Ministry

Marriage is a ministry that serves God's kingdom. When two people unite in marriage, they are called to serve one another and the world around them. Married couples can be powerful witnesses to the world by showing what

Christ-like love looks like in action. A godly marriage can inspire others to seek Christ and experience His love and grace.

> *"In the same way, let your light shine before others, that they may see your good deeds and glorify your Father in heaven."*
>
> *Matthew 5:16 (NIV)*

Partnership in Fulfilling God's Calling

God often calls married couples to fulfil specific purposes together. The unity between husband and wife is meant to amplify their ability to serve God. A godly marriage can provide the support, encouragement, and strength needed to carry out God's calling, whether in ministry, missions, or everyday life. When both partners are aligned in their faith and values, their marriage becomes a powerful partnership for advancing God's kingdom.

Marriage as a Reflection of God's Divine Purpose

God's intentions for marriage are far greater than personal happiness or societal expectations. Marriage is a covenant that reflects the very nature of God — His love, faithfulness, and desire for unity. It serves a higher purpose in God's plan, including companionship, procreation, spiritual growth, and the advancement of His kingdom on earth.

When couples align their marriage with God's design, they not only experience deeper fulfilment but also become a reflection of Christ's love for the world. By prioritising spiritual growth, sacrificial love, and mutual submission, Christian marriages can stand as a testament to the transformative power of God's love, fulfilling His purpose for creation and reflecting His glory.

Finding a life partner is about more than just companionship, romance, or shared interests. It is about aligning with someone who complements your life's purpose and journey and supporting each other in living out God's plan. As Christians, it is vital to approach relationships with intentionality, keeping in mind how a partner can help you fulfil your unique calling and how you can do the same for them.

It is important therefore, that you know your purpose and calling. Here's how you can know yourself before knowing someone else

Before seeking a partner, it is essential to have a clear understanding of who you are. Self-awareness is foundational to a healthy and God-honouring relationship. Taking the time to evaluate your spiritual, emotional, and personal readiness will prepare you for a meaningful and purposeful partnership.

What is My Relationship with God?

The cornerstone of any successful Christian relationship is a strong personal relationship with God. Matthew 6:33 reminds us, "*But seek first his kingdom and his righteousness, and all these things will be given to you as well.*" Before seeking a life partner, evaluate your spiritual health. Are you growing in your faith and walking closely with the Lord? A thriving relationship with God ensures that you are building your life on a firm foundation.

Practical Steps:

- *Establish a daily devotional routine to deepen your spiritual intimacy.*
- *Join a small group or Bible study to grow in community and accountability.*
- *Volunteer in ministry to align your life with God's purpose and serve others.*

What Are My Core Values and Non-Negotiables?

Understanding your core values and what you consider non-negotiable is vital for building a relationship rooted in unity. Amos 3:3 poses the question, *"Can two walk together unless they are agreed?"* Shared values such as faith, integrity, family, and purpose, are essential for long-term compatibility.

Take time to define your values and ensure they align with biblical principles. Non-negotiables might include a shared faith in Christ, honesty, commitment to family, or a willingness to grow spiritually.

Practical Steps

- *Write down your core values and pray over them.*
- *Reflect on what traits or beliefs are most important in a partner.*
- *Assess whether your non-negotiables are rooted in God's Word or shaped by cultural expectations.*

Am I Emotionally and Mentally Ready for Marriage?

Marriage is a union that requires maturity, patience, and resilience. Proverbs 4:23 advises, "*Above all else, guard your heart, for everything you do flows from it.*" It is important to evaluate whether you have addressed any emotional wounds, past relationships, or unresolved issues that could hinder your ability to build a healthy marriage.

Emotional and mental readiness involve self-awareness, forgiving past hurts, and communicating effectively. Marriage is not about finding someone to complete you but about two individuals coming together to complement each other.

Practical Steps

- *Reflect on past relationships or experiences that need healing or closure.*
- *Seek counselling, mentorship, or prayer to address unresolved trauma or insecurities.*
- *Develop emotional intelligence by learning to express feelings and handle conflict gracefully.*

Knowing yourself is the first step in preparing for a God-honouring relationship. By focusing on your spiritual growth, defining your values, and addressing emotional readiness, you create a strong foundation for a partnership that reflects Christ's love and purpose. Only when you know who you are in Christ can you truly seek and nurture a relationship that aligns with God's plan?

Here are some things to reflect on concerning your life purpose and how a partner can complement that journey.

Discover Your Life Purpose, So You'd Attract The Right Companion for Your Journey

Before thinking about a relationship, it's important to understand your life purpose. Each of us is created by God with unique gifts, passions, and callings. As Ephesians 2:10 says:

> "*For we are God's handiwork, created in Christ Jesus to do good works, which God prepared in advance for us to do.*"
>
> *Ephesians 2:10 (NIV)*

Ask yourselves the following questions to begin uncovering your purpose:

- *What are my God-given gifts and talents?*
- *Reflect on the areas where you naturally excel and find joy. God often calls us to use our strengths to serve others.*
- *What are your passions?*
- *What stirs your heart? Your passions can be a strong indicator of where God is calling you to serve.*
- *What burden has God placed on your heart?*

Sometimes, our life purpose is tied to a specific need or problem we feel called to address, whether it's in ministry, social justice, teaching, healthcare, or another field.

How is God currently working in your life?

Reflect on the experiences, opportunities, and challenges you've faced. These often prepare and shape us for our purpose.

It's essential to pray about these questions, seeking God's guidance as you discern your calling. Being clear on your purpose makes it easier to identify a partner who will complement that journey, rather than distract from it.

Understand That Marriage Is a Partnership in God's Plan

Once you have a clearer sense of your life purpose, it's important to think about how marriage can play a role in that calling. Marriage, when aligned with God's plan, is more than just a personal relationship; it's a spiritual partnership. Together, couples can amplify each other's ability to serve and grow in their God-given missions. Consider the following:

Mutual Encouragement and Support

A good partner will encourage you to pursue your God-given purpose, offering support and advice along the way. Ecclesiastes 4:9-10 reminds us:

> *"Two are better than one, because they have a good return for their labor: If either of them falls down, one can help the other up."*
>
> *Ecclesiastes 4:9-10 (NIV)*

This scripture highlights the power of partnership—how working together produces greater results and provides strength when challenges arise. In marriage, each partner should build the other up, helping them to fulfil their calling while receiving the same support in return.

Complementary Strengths

Look for someone whose strengths complement yours. If your purpose involves leadership or entrepreneurship, a partner with strong organisational skills and emotional intelligence might be a great fit. If you feel called to missionary work, you'll need a partner who shares or supports that vision, even if it requires sacrifices. It's not about finding someone identical to you but someone whose gifts and character enhance your journey.

As 1 Corinthians 12:12 says:

> *"Just as a body, though one, has many parts, but all its many parts form one body, so it is with Christ."*
>
> *1 Corinthians 12:12 (NIV)*

In marriage, each partner brings unique gifts, and together they can form a powerful unit that better serves God's plan.

Shared Values and Mission

A shared sense of mission is crucial for a lasting partnership. Couples need to be united in their vision for life and service. This doesn't mean that both individuals must have the same job or role, but they should share core values about what matters most – living for God, serving others, and building a Christ-centred life. A Bible verse asks:

> *"Can two walk together unless they agree?"*
>
> *Amos 3:3 (NKJV)*

A strong partnership thrives when both individuals are aligned in their long-term vision. Reflect on whether a potential partner shares your priorities—both in the present and for the future—and invite them to consider the deeper layers of compatibility. While immediate chemistry or shared interests are important, long-term compatibility often hinges on aligning values, goals, and visions for life. Here's an expanded perspective:

Define Your Core Priorities First

Before evaluating a partner's alignment, one must have clarity on their values, aspirations, and non-negotiables. Ask yourself:

- *What do I value most in life (e.g., career, family, personal growth, faith)?*
- *What kind of lifestyle do I envision (e.g., urban or rural living, financial goals, parenting style)?*
- *What are my long-term dreams, and how much am I willing to compromise?*

Clarity in these areas makes it easier to assess whether a potential partner's life direction complements your own.

Look Beyond Surface-Level Compatibility

Initial attraction often revolves around shared hobbies, humour, or physical chemistry. While these are essential for connection, deeper alignment lies in shared visions for the future. For instance:

- *Does the person share the same vision as you? For example, if you prioritise building a family, does your partner share that vision?*
- *Does the person support you and does their goals align with the sacrifices it may envisage? For example, If you are driven by professional ambition, Will the person be in support of this, and do their goals align with the sacrifices it may entail?*
- *Do your views on finances, work-life balance, and travel mesh well?*

Discuss the Big Questions Early

Engage in honest conversations about key aspects of life direction. While timing is sensitive, deeper discussions build a stronger foundation. Here are some questions to explore:

- *How do you imagine your life in 5, 10, or 20 years?*

- *What roles do relationships, careers, children, or personal development play in your ideal future?*
- *How do you approach change and challenges in life?*

A willingness to have these conversations reveals emotional maturity and a readiness for partnership.

Observe and Reflect on Actions

Words are important, but actions speak louder. Does the person's behaviour reflect shared priorities? For example:

If financial stability is important to you, are they making decisions that reflect responsibility?

If personal growth is a mutual priority, do they actively pursue learning and self-improvement?

If health and fitness matter, are they aligned in lifestyle choices?

Their consistent actions over time will reveal alignment or divergence.

Account for Growth and Flexibility

While shared priorities are critical, so is the ability to adapt as life evolves. A great partner doesn't just match your current priorities, they also share the capacity to grow alongside you:

- *Are they open to adjusting shared goals as circumstances change?*
- *Do they exhibit emotional resilience and the ability to navigate life's uncertainties?*
- *Are they supportive of your growth, even if it requires some realignment?*

Recognise Potential Deal-Breakers Early

Not every mismatch in priorities is reconcilable. Reflecting early can help identify areas where alignment is unlikely:

A partner who strongly desires a child-free life may not align with your dream of a big family. Differences in religious beliefs, if central to one person's identity, can create significant challenges. Acknowledging these gaps early prevents heartbreak and fosters the pursuit of more compatible connections.

Leverage Shared Goals to Strengthen Bonds

When priorities align, use this common ground as a foundation for collaboration and support. Shared vision fosters teamwork and mutual encouragement:

Plan together for shared goals (e.g., saving for a home, career transitions).

Celebrate milestones as you make progress toward mutual dreams.

Focusing on alignment in priorities not only ensures long-term compatibility but also strengthens the relationship's foundation, making it more resilient to life's inevitable ups and downs. By reflecting deeply and acting intentionally, individuals can build connections rooted in a shared vision of the future. Here are some key questions to think about when considering how your intending partner complements your life purpose:

What are the core values you want your life to reflect?

Whether it's integrity, generosity, serving others, or a deep commitment to faith, it's important to know what principles guide your life and if a potential partner shares those values.

How do I want to serve God with my life?

Consider the type of ministry, career, or calling that excites you. Does your partner encourage that, and are they interested in being part of that journey? Will you both encourage each other's spiritual growth and service to God?

Can this relationship help me grow closer to God?

Spiritual growth is the cornerstone of any Christian relationship. Does your partner challenge you to grow in your faith, pursue godliness, and become more like Christ?

Do we have a shared vision for the future?

While people can have different careers or interests, a shared long-term vision is crucial for building a strong, purposeful marriage. Discuss goals for ministry, family, lifestyle, and how you both see yourselves making an impact in the world for God's kingdom.

How to Choose a Partner Who Aligns with Your Purpose

The Bible teaches that the right partner will help you fulfil your God-given purpose and vice versa. Proverbs 31:10 speaks to the value of finding a partner of noble character:

> *"A wife of noble character who can find? She is worth far more than rubies."*
>
> *Proverbs 31:10 (NIV)*

This applies equally to husbands. A noble partner—one who loves God, shares your values, and is committed to living a life of purpose—is invaluable in the journey of life. This enables you to avoid future misalignment of goals and ultimate regret. So, seek a partner who:

- *Prioritises their relationship with God*

- *A partner who is grounded in faith will naturally complement your journey by fostering a spiritual environment that honours God.*
- *Shares similar life goals and values*
- *Whether it's ministry, raising a family, or serving others, a shared purpose builds unity in marriage.*
- *Encourages your growth and challenges you to pursue God's will*
- *A partner who challenges you spiritually, emotionally, and personally helps you fulfil your purpose in ways you couldn't on your own.*

Practical Tips for Reflection

Spend time in prayer: Ask God for wisdom and clarity about your life purpose and what kind of partner would best complement that journey.

Seek wise counsel: Talk to mentors, spiritual leaders, or trusted friends who can offer guidance as you reflect on your purpose and how a relationship fits into that picture.

Be patient: God's timing is perfect. Sometimes, the season of singleness is meant for self-discovery and preparation. Don't rush finding a partner—allow God to shape you and your future spouse.

Act in your purpose now: Don't wait for a partner to start living out your purpose. Step into what God is calling you to do now, trusting that the right partner will complement your journey in time.

A Partner as a Catalyst for Purpose

A godly partner is someone you love and who walks alongside you in fulfilling God's purpose for your life. By reflecting on your life's calling and praying for a partner who complements that journey, you are setting the foundation for a marriage that honours God, serves His kingdom, and makes a lasting impact on the world. A life partner should amplify your mission. When two people are united in a shared purpose under God, their marriage becomes a powerful testimony of His love and grace.

2

Preparing Your Heart And Mind

This chapter emphasises the importance of developing a strong relationship with God first, trusting that He will provide the right partner at the right time.

Sarah's Story

Sarah is a young woman who has experienced multiple failed relationships. Each time, she believed she had found the right person, only to be left heartbroken. After her third breakup, she realised the problem wasn't just the men she was dating but her unresolved issues with trust and self-worth. She began focusing on her relationship with God, spending time in prayer and scripture, asking for healing and guidance. As Sarah allowed herself to heal, she realised that her desire for a relationship was more about filling a void than finding a God-centred partner.

Preparing Your Heart and Mind

Before you can choose the right partner, you need to prepare yourself emotionally, spiritually, and mentally. This chapter dives into the importance of healing past wounds and letting go of emotional baggage from previous relationships. Many people enter relationships with unresolved hurt, which can hinder their ability to form a healthy connection.

Preparing your heart and mind for choosing the right partner is a journey that requires intentionality, prayer, and trust in God. As you focus on strengthening your relationship with God, healing from past hurts, and clarifying your values, you create a solid foundation for a future relationship built on mutual respect, love, and faith. Trust in God's perfect plan and timing, knowing that He is guiding you toward the partner who will complement your life and help you grow in His love.

Remember, the process of choosing a partner is not just about finding the right person—it's about becoming the right person for someone else. Let God work in your heart as you prepare for the beautiful future He has in store for you.

Self-reflecting through journaling, A key to Preparation

Singles, you need to prepare your mind and heart by engaging in self-reflection by journaling. Writing your thoughts is a most effective way to track and analyse your intentions and actions. Journaling is a powerful tool for personal growth and spiritual reflection. When it comes to relationships—whether you're single, dating, or preparing for marriage—taking the time to journal about your desires, expectations, and past experiences can provide clarity and help align your heart with God's will. It allows you to step back and prayerfully assess where you've been, what you're hoping for, and how God is guiding your path toward the right partner.

Here's why and how journaling can be a transformative practice on your journey toward finding a godly relationship.

1. Clarity on Your Desires and Expectations

It's natural to have hopes and expectations when it comes to relationships, but it's important to ensure that these are rooted in biblical truths rather than cultural pressures or personal fears. Journaling helps you clarify what you truly desire in a partner and marriage. It forces you to ask hard questions about what matters most to you in a relationship.

Reflect on questions such as:

- *What are my non-negotiables in a relationship?*
- *Consider your core values and spiritual beliefs. What aspects of your faith, lifestyle, or future goals do you need your partner to share? Write down qualities that are essential to a godly relationship.*
- *What are my hopes for marriage?*
- *Are you seeking a relationship that centres on faith and service? How do you envision your future family or ministry together? Journaling allows you to dream about your future with God's purpose in mind.*
- *What expectations do I have about love and marriage?*

Expectations can sometimes be unrealistic or unspoken, which can lead to disappointment. Writing them out helps you recognise which ones are healthy and rooted in God's Word and which ones might need adjustment.

2. Processing Past Relationships

One of the most valuable things journaling can offer is the ability to process past relationships and learn from them. Whether you've experienced heartbreak, disappointment, or confusion, journaling gives you a safe space to explore what went wrong, what you learned, and how God used those experiences to shape you.

In processing past relationships, ask such questions as:

What have I learned from past relationships?

Evaluate your previous relationships, identifying patterns that might need to change or lessons that were learned. Were there red flags you ignored? Did you compromise on your values? Writing it all down allows you to see things more clearly.

What wounds do I need to heal from?

If a past relationship caused emotional or spiritual harm, journaling can be a way to bring those wounds to God for healing. Be honest about the pain you've experienced and allow the journaling process to lead you to forgiveness and closure, with the help of prayer and reflection.

Where did I see God's hand in my past relationships?

Even in failed relationships, God is always present. Reflect on how God was working, whether it was through guiding you away from the wrong person or teaching you to trust Him more deeply.

3. Aligning Your Desires with God's Will

Journaling isn't just about self-reflection; it's also a way to connect more deeply with God and seek His guidance. As you write out your desires for a relationship and marriage, take the time to ask God if these desires align with His will. Journaling allows you to surrender your hopes to God and seek His wisdom in shaping them.

Good prayer direction while you self reflect are listed below:

"Lord, help me to see my relationships through Your eyes."

Ask God to give you clarity and discernment when it comes to relationships. Use journaling to pour out your heart to Him, trusting that He will guide you.

"God, align my desires with Your plan."

Sometimes, we hold onto desires that are based on worldly ideals rather than God's perfect plan for us. Journaling gives you space to submit those desires to Him and ask for alignment with His purpose.

"Father, show me how to be the partner You've called me to be."

It's easy to focus on what we want from someone else, but journaling helps us reflect on how we can grow into the person God wants us to be for our future spouse. Writing out your thoughts can reveal areas where God is working in your life to make you a better partner.

4. Creating Space for Gratitude and Growth

Journaling not only helps you process past hurts or clarify desires but also cultivates gratitude for the journey you're on. Take time to reflect on what God has already done in your life—how He has protected you, grown you, and led you toward a greater understanding of His will for your relationships.

Here are some great themes to journal about:

Moments of growth and wisdom

What lessons have you learned through singleness, past relationships, or dating? Write about how God has used each season of your life to refine you.

Ways God has protected or blessed you

Even if you haven't met the right person yet, reflect on how God has kept you from the wrong situations or relationships. Gratitude shifts your perspective, reminding you that God is working for your good, even when you can't see it.

Current blessings in your life

It's easy to become fixated on finding the right partner, but journaling allows you to see the beauty and blessings in your current season. Write down things you're grateful for in your singleness or dating life, focusing on how God is using this time to prepare you for what's ahead.

5. Practical Journaling Prompts for Relationship Reflection

If you're new to journaling or need help getting started, here are some practical prompts to guide your reflections:

What top five values do I want my relationship to reflect?

This prompt will encourage you to think about your priorities and how you want your future relationship to honour God and your convictions.

In what ways have I grown through my past relationships?

Reflecting on growth helps you see how God has used your experiences to prepare you for the right partner.

What qualities do I believe God wants me to look for in a partner?

This prompt challenges you to think biblically and prayerfully about what truly matters in a relationship, focusing on character, faith, and purpose over superficial traits.

How can I better prepare myself to be the kind of spouse I desire to have?

Instead of only thinking about what you want in a partner, reflect on how God is shaping you to be the partner someone else is praying for.

What fears or worries do I need to surrender to God about relationships?

Journaling can help you bring your anxieties to the surface, allowing you to release them to God and trust His plan.

6. Using Journaling to Track Your Faith Journey

Finally, journaling is a way to track your faith journey around relationships. Over time, as you look back at your entries, you'll be able to see how God has been faithful, how your desires and expectations have matured, and how you've grown as a person.

Track your Journal:

Regularly revisit old entries: Go back and read past journal entries to see how God has answered prayers or worked in your life. This can build your faith and remind you of His abiding presence.

Set aside time for journaling consistently: Whether weekly or monthly, make journaling a regular practice to reflect on what God is teaching you about relationships, life purpose, and His plans for your future.

Include scripture in your journaling: Incorporate Bible verses that resonate with your reflections. For example, if you're writing about your hopes for the future, you might include Jeremiah 29:11, trusting in God's plans for you.

Journaling as a Path to Greater Clarity and Faith

Writing a journal concerning your desires, expectations, and past experiences creates space for self-discovery, healing, and spiritual growth. As you reflect on your journey, you'll gain insight into who you are, what God is calling you to, and how a partner can complement that path. Journaling becomes a way to connect more deeply with God, inviting His wisdom and direction into life's most important decisions—including relationships.

In the end, as people trust God with their future, they'll find greater peace in waiting for the right person, knowing that God's hand is shaping their desires and expectations. Ask guiding questions like:

What do I truly want in a partner?

What are my non-negotiables?

Healing Past Wounds: Emotional Healing and Choosing the Right Partner

Finding the right partner is not just about compatibility; it's about entering a relationship as whole and healed individuals, ready to give and receive love in a healthy way. Unresolved pain from past relationships can create barriers to trust, communication, and intimacy. Emotional healing is essential to ensure your future relationship is built on a foundation of grace, understanding, and love.

Why Emotional Healing Matters

It Helps to Prevents Carrying Emotional Baggage: Without healing, the pain of past relationships can distort how you view your new partner.

It Builds Emotional Maturity: Healing helps you approach relationships with clarity, free from bitterness or fear.

It Helps You to Reflect God's Design for Wholeness: God calls us to find rest and renewal in Him so that we can move forward unburdened (Matthew 11:28-30).

> "*Come to me, all who labor and are heavy laden, and I will give you rest. Take my yoke upon you, and learn from me, for I am gentle and lowly in heart, and you will find rest for your souls. For my yoke is easy, and my burden is light.*"

Steps for Forgiveness, Moving Forward, and Self-Care

1. Acknowledge the Hurt

Be honest with yourself about the pain you feel. Avoid minimising your emotions or pretending they don't exist. Pray for wisdom and clarity to understand how past relationships have impacted you.

2. Surrender the Pain to God

Spend time in prayer, asking God to help you release the burden of hurt and anger.

Meditate on Matthew 11:28-30, trusting Jesus to provide rest for your weary soul.

3. Forgive Others and Yourself

Forgiveness is not condoning what happened but releasing yourself from its control.

Write a letter (even if you don't send it) to express forgiveness to the person who hurt you.

Forgive yourself for mistakes you've made and accept God's grace.

4. Practice Self-Care

Prioritise activities that nurture your mind, body, and soul.

Sleep: Get consistent, restorative sleep to help your emotional balance.

Nutrition: Eat foods that fuel your body and mind.

Relaxation: Incorporate activities like reading, journaling, or prayerful meditation to reduce stress.

Take time to do things you love, whether it's a hobby, creative pursuit, or quiet moments with God.

5. Commit to Regular Exercise

Exercise helps release stress, boosts mood, and improves overall well-being.

Engage in physical activities like walking, running, yoga, or strength training at least 3–4 times a week.

Use your exercise time to pray, reflect, or listen to uplifting worship music. As 1 Corinthians 6:19-20 reminds us, our bodies are temples of the Holy Spirit—caring for them honours God.

6. Seek Wisdom Through God's Word

Let Scripture renew your mind and help you understand God's design for love and relationships.

Focus on verses like Ephesians 4:31-32: "Let all bitterness and wrath and anger and clamour and slander be put away from you, along with all malice. Be kind to one another, tender hearted, forgiving one another, as God in Christ forgave you."

7. Take Time for Personal Growth

Use this season to grow emotionally, spiritually, and mentally. Develop healthy habits and deepen your relationship with God. Reflect on what you've learned from past relationships to avoid repeating patterns.

8. Trust in God's Timing

Don't rush into a new relationship to fill a void. Trust that God will bring the right partner at the right time.

Proverbs 3:5-6 reminds us:

> "*Trust in the Lord with all your heart, and do not lean on your own understanding. In all your ways acknowledge him, and he will make straight your paths.*"

Moving Forward

Healing takes time, but with God's help, you can let go of the past and embrace a hopeful future. Commit to self-care and emotional renewal, trusting that as you care for yourself, you're preparing your heart and life for the partner God has for you. When you approach a new relationship from a place of wholeness—physically, emotionally, and spiritually—you're better equipped to love and be loved in the way God intended.

Let His peace guide your steps, and trust that He is writing your love story in His perfect time.

3

Identifying Godly Qualities In A Partner

This chapter covers the practical aspects of what to look for in a partner, focusing on values, character, and faith. Godly qualities such as honesty, kindness, emotional maturity, and shared faith form the foundation of a strong relationship.

Sarah's journey of faith led her to understand that chemistry wasn't enough. In her past relationships, she often prioritised physical attraction and the emotional high of being in love, without evaluating the deeper aspects of her partner's character. As she matured spiritually, she began praying for God to show her what to look for in a future spouse.

Identifying Godly Qualities in a Partner

As a single person, it is essential to approach the idea of a life partner with intentionality, prayer, and a clear understanding of what qualities truly matter. In choosing a partner, the focus should not only be on superficial traits but, more importantly, on godly qualities that align with God's Word and His purposes for relationships. A godly partner will help you grow in your faith, build a Christ-centred life together, and honour God through mutual love and respect. Below are key godly qualities to look for when identifying a potential partner:

Key Qualities:

Honesty and Integrity: A partner should be truthful, transparent, and reliable. Without trust, a relationship cannot thrive.

Kindness and Compassion: True love reflects God's unconditional love, and a potential partner should exhibit genuine care for others, particularly their intended life partner.

Emotional Maturity: Look for someone who handles conflicts and challenges with grace, someone who can communicate openly without defensiveness or shutting down.

Shared Faith and Values: A relationship rooted in shared faith provides a solid spiritual foundation, allowing both partners to grow together in their walk with God.

Character Over Chemistry: Danger

Short-Term Infatuation vs. Long-Term Compatibility

Description

Physical attraction fades over time; without shared values, relationships struggle to endure.

Illustrative Story

Emily fell for Jason's charm and good looks but ignored red flags like his lack of commitment and dismissive attitude. When their initial chemistry faded, constant arguments over values and priorities led to their breakup.

Lesson

Relationships built solely on physical attraction often crumble under real-life challenges.

Character Over Chemistry: Danger

Overlooking Character Flaws

Description

Focusing on looks can blind you to harmful traits or toxic behaviours

Illustrative Story

David stayed with Claire because of her stunning appearance, even though she frequently belittled him and others. Over time, her lack of kindness and respect eroded his self-esteem, and he eventually ended the relationship.

Lesson

Ignoring toxic traits in favour of physical appeal can harm emotional well-being.

Character Over Chemistry: Danger

Misjudging Compatibility

Description

Mismatched values and goals create conflicts that attraction alone can't resolve.

Illustrative Story

Sophia was captivated by Marcus's looks but soon realised they had different priorities. She valued family, while Marcus preferred a carefree lifestyle. Their conflicts over future goals eventually drove them apart.

Lesson

Physical attraction can't bridge gaps in values and life goals.

Character Over Chemistry: Danger

Ignoring Inner Beauty

Description

By prioritising physical attraction, you may overlook someone with strong character and compatibility.

Illustrative Story

Ryan dismissed Emma because she didn't fit his ideal image, despite their shared values and interests. After failed relationships with more "attractive" partners, he realised he had missed out on a meaningful connection with Emma.

Lesson

Judging solely on appearance may lead you to miss fulfilling relationships.

Character Over Chemistry: Danger

Superficial Relationships and Loneliness

Description

Relationships based only on looks often lack emotional depth, leading to loneliness.

Illustrative Story

Lila was thrilled to date Alex, a fitness model, but felt isolated when he showed no interest in her personal struggles. His focus on image over emotional connection made her feel lonelier in the relationship than when she was single.

Lesson

Emotional connection is vital for a fulfilling relationship.

Character Over Chemistry: Danger

Increased Vulnerability to Manipulation

Description

Placing too much value on looks can make you susceptible to manipulation or power imbalances.

Illustrative Story

Jake compromised on everything to keep Samantha, who used her looks to control the relationship. Friends warned him of the unhealthy dynamic, but it wasn't until he felt emotionally drained that he ended things

Lesson

Superficial priorities can lead to power imbalances and exploitation.

While physical attraction is important, prioritising character ensures deeper emotional connections and long-lasting compatibility. By balancing physical appeal with inner qualities like integrity, kindness, and shared values, relationships can thrive beyond the initial spark.

Godly Qualities to Look for in a Spouse

The Bible provides timeless principles about the character and qualities to seek in a partner:

1. A Genuine Relationship with God

Look for someone who loves God wholeheartedly. 2 Corinthians 6:14 warns against being "yoked together with unbelievers." A shared faith is the foundation for spiritual harmony. Observe their commitment to spiritual disciplines like prayer, church attendance, and serving others.

2. Godly Character

Traits like kindness, humility, patience, and integrity are essential (Colossians 3:12-14). Avoid being swayed solely by outward appearances (1 Samuel 16:7).

Evaluate how they treat others, especially in challenging situations. Do they demonstrate the fruit of the Spirit (Galatians 5:22-23)?

3. A Spirit of Service

Does this person reflect Christ's love through serving others? Philippians 2:3-4 teaches us to value others above ourselves, an attitude vital in marriage.

Consider how they handle opportunities to help others. Are they willing to sacrifice their own comfort for the benefit of those in need?

4. Emotional and Financial Stewardship

A responsible and mature partner should demonstrate wise management of emotions and resources (Proverbs 21:5). Assess their approach to handling finances. Do they plan wisely and avoid unnecessary debt? Financial disagreements can strain a marriage, so it's essential to align spending and saving habits.

Shared Values and Beliefs:

The Importance of Shared Values in Relationships

Shared values, especially concerning faith and life priorities, are foundational for building strong, lasting relationships. **2 Corinthians 6:14** emphasises this principle: "*Do not be yoked together with unbelievers. For what do righteousness and wickedness have in common? Or what fellowship can light have with darkness?*" This passage highlights the spiritual and practical challenges of partnering with someone whose core beliefs and life goals differ from your own.

When couples align on values, particularly in areas like faith and life priorities, they build a relationship that fosters unity, mutual understanding, and a shared sense of purpose. Here's why shared values matter and how singles can effectively assess compatibility.

Why Shared Values Are Essential

1. Unified Direction in Life

Couples with shared values move toward a common vision. This is especially true in faith-based relationships, where shared beliefs influence how partners make decisions, raise children, and handle challenges. A mismatch in values can create division and conflict.

2. Stronger Emotional Connection

Shared values deepen emotional intimacy by fostering mutual respect and understanding. When both partners prioritise similar principles—such as faith, honesty, or service—it strengthens the bond.

3. Resilience Through Challenges

Life inevitably brings trials, and having shared values equips couples to face them together. A shared faith, for example, provides spiritual grounding and hope during difficult seasons.

4. Clarity in Decision-Making

Core values influence decisions on major topics like finances, career goals, parenting, and lifestyle. Aligning in these areas minimises misunderstandings and promotes harmony.

5. Spiritual Growth

When faith is central to both partners, they can encourage each other's spiritual growth, pray together, and seek God's will as a team.

Key Questions to Assess Compatibility

Faith-Based Questions

- Do you share the same foundational beliefs about God, salvation, and the role of faith in daily life?
- How important is prayer, worship, and church community in your individual lives and potential life together?
- Are you aligned on your willingness to integrate faith into parenting, finances, and decision-making?

- Do you agree on the importance of spiritual growth and accountability in your relationship?

Life Priority Questions

- What are your long-term goals for your career, family, and lifestyle? Are they compatible?
- How do you define success, and what role do faith and values play in achieving it?
- Are you aligned on financial priorities, such as saving, giving, and spending?
- How do you approach conflict resolution, forgiveness, and communication?
- What are your views on work-life balance, and how do they reflect our values?

Practical Relationship Questions

- How do you feel about community involvement, generosity, and serving others?
- Do you agree on how to spend time together and apart (e.g., hobbies, family involvement)?

- Are you open to compromise and growth when your priorities evolve?
- What non-negotiable values do you each hold, and are they aligned?

Why This Matters

Avoiding Division:

As 2 Corinthians 6:14 warns, being "unequally yoked" can lead to tension and division. If one partner prioritises faith and the other dismisses its significance, disagreements on major life issues can arise.

Building a Legacy

Shared values create a foundation for leaving a positive legacy—whether through raising children with shared principles, influencing others with your relationship, or serving together for a greater purpose.

Honouring God in the Relationship

A relationship rooted in shared faith glorifies God. It reflects mutual obedience to His Word and the pursuit of His will as a couple.

Minimizing Regret

A mismatch in values can result in long-term frustration, heartbreak, or feelings of compromise. Aligning on what matters most ensures confidence in the relationship's future.

Actionable Steps

1. **Pray for Wisdom**: Seek God's guidance in understanding your values and discerning compatibility with a potential partner.
2. **Have Honest Conversations**: Early discussions about faith and life priorities help set the tone for authenticity and alignment.
3. **Observe Actions**: A person's lifestyle and decisions often reveal their true values more clearly than words.

4. **Seek Counsel**: Trusted friends, mentors, or spiritual leaders can provide insight into whether your relationship aligns with Biblical principles.

Shared values, especially around faith and life priorities, are essential for a thriving, God-honouring relationship. By prioritising alignment in these areas, you can build partnerships that endure life's challenges, foster spiritual growth, and create a legacy of love and faith. Use the questions above as a guide to evaluate compatibility and ensure that your relationship is rooted in what truly matters.

Why Shared Values Around Faith and Life Priorities Matter

1. Guides Decision-Making

Shared faith and values provide a consistent moral and ethical framework, guiding decisions in finances, parenting, and relationships. Couples who align in these areas often experience smoother communication and mutual understanding.

2. Builds Emotional and Spiritual Intimacy

Spiritual practices, like prayer or worship, foster emotional and spiritual intimacy. When both partners share the same faith, they can grow closer through shared rituals and values.

3. Reduces Conflict

Differing values about priorities like career, family, or personal growth can lead to significant conflicts. Shared values help couples approach challenges with similar perspectives and avoid unnecessary strife.

4. Creates a Unified Vision for the Future

Shared faith and aligned life goals ensure that both partners are working toward the same vision, whether it's raising children in a specific faith, pursuing similar financial goals, or committing to a particular lifestyle.

5. Prepares Couples for Adversity

When tough times come, a shared faith can provide strength and hope. Partners can support each other spiritually, lean on shared beliefs, and trust in the same higher power.

The Power of Unity in Shared Values

Couples who are "equally yoked" share not only faith but also a commitment to aligning their life priorities. While differences in personality or interests can enrich a relationship, shared values act as a compass, ensuring both partners are heading in the same direction.

By having open, honest discussions and prayerfully considering compatibility, couples can build a relationship rooted in mutual respect, love, and shared purpose. This alignment honours God's design for unity in relationships and provides a firm foundation for a lasting partnership.

Key Qualities to Look For:

Honesty and Integrity:

Honesty and integrity are cornerstones of a strong and healthy relationship. They build trust, foster open communication, and create a safe environment where both partners can thrive. Here are examples of what honesty and integrity look like in real-life situations:

1. Transparency About Feelings

This shows emotional honesty and respects the partner's right to understand what's going on in the relationship.

2. Owning Up to Mistakes

Taking responsibility for mistakes shows accountability and a commitment to repairing trust.

3. Consistency Between Words and Actions

Acting in alignment with one's promises builds trust and demonstrates reliability.

4. Speaking Up When Something Feels Wrong

Being honest about concerns, even when it's uncomfortable, shows integrity and care for the relationship's well-being.

5. Respecting Boundaries and Agreements

Honouring agreements reflect respect and reliability, which are key components of integrity.

6. Being Honest About Expectations

Honesty about major life goals prevents misunderstandings and ensures both partners are on the same page.

7. Admitting Vulnerabilities

Being honest about personal struggles fosters emotional intimacy and trust.

8. Not Hiding Financial Matters

Transparency about finances demonstrates integrity and a willingness to address challenges as a team.

9. Standing Up for the Relationship

Integrity involves loyalty, even when the partner isn't present, and reinforces trust in the relationship.

10. Refusing to Engage in Deception

Choosing honesty over deception, even in small matters, strengthens trust and avoids unnecessary conflict.

Why These Behaviours Matter

Builds Trust:

Consistently being honest and acting with integrity fosters a strong foundation of trust.

Promotes Mutual Respect:

Honesty shows that both partners value and respect each other's thoughts, feelings, and boundaries.

Encourages Growth:

Integrity helps couples navigate challenges together, fostering deeper understanding and resilience.

By embodying honesty and integrity, couples create an environment where both partners feel secure, valued, and understood, paving the way for a strong and lasting relationship.

Kindness and Compassion:

Observing how someone treats others can offer profound insights into their character. Acts of kindness and compassion toward people outside the relationship—such as strangers, friends, family, or service workers—are often indicators of how they will treat you in the long run. These observations reveal the depth of their empathy, respect, and values.

Why a Partner's Treatment of Others Matters

1. Reflects Authenticity

How someone behaves when they have no incentive to impress (e.g., toward strangers or those they don't "need") reveals their true nature. A partner who consistently demonstrates kindness likely has an authentic, caring heart.

2. Predicts How They Will Treat You Over Time

Initial romantic gestures may fade as the relationship settles, but their habitual treatment of others provides a glimpse of how they'll act toward you when the "honeymoon phase" ends.

3. Shows Respect for All People

A compassionate partner values human dignity and equality. If they treat everyone with respect, it's a sign they understand and uphold the importance of treating loved ones well.

4. Demonstrates Emotional Maturity

Kindness and compassion often come from emotional maturity and self-awareness. A partner who responds with patience and grace under stress is more likely to foster a healthy relationship.

5. Reveals Core Values

How someone treats others reflects their moral compass. A person committed to kindness is likely guided by values that align with creating a loving, supportive partnership.

Examples of Behaviours to Observe

Situation	What to Look For
Interactions with Workers	Are they polite, patient, and respectful? Do they say "thank you" or treat workers dismissively, especially when things don't go perfectly?
Conflict with Others	How do they handle disagreements? Are they calm and solution-focused, or do they resort to insults, anger, or manipulation?
Acts of Generosity	Do they offer help to those in need, whether it's a friend, family member, or stranger? Are they willing to inconvenience themselves to assist others?
Relationship with Family	How do they speak about and interact with their family? Do they show respect and appreciation, or are they dismissive and critical?

Treatment of Animals	Are they gentle and considerate with animals? Cruelty or indifference to animals can be a red flag for a lack of empathy.
Reactions to Vulnerability	How do they respond when someone else is in distress? Do they show empathy and offer support, or are they indifferent or judgmental?
Handling Mistakes	If someone else makes an error (e.g., a server gets their order wrong), are they understanding and forgiving, or do they react with frustration or anger?

Red Flags to Watch For

1. Rudeness to Workers or Strangers

Disrespect or entitlement toward those in service roles indicates a lack of empathy and compassion.

2. Inconsistent Kindness

Being kind only to people who are "useful" or in positions of power suggests conditional, self-serving behaviour.

3. Speaking Poorly of Others Behind Their Backs

Gossiping or being overly critical of others reflects insecurity and a tendency toward negativity.

4. Aggression During Conflict

Explosive or demeaning responses during disagreements show a lack of self-control and respect.

Questions to Reflect On

- How does this person treat people who can't "benefit" them in any way?
- Do they display consistent kindness, even when stressed or inconvenienced?
- How do they handle situations where someone is vulnerable or in need?
- Are their acts of compassion genuine, or do they seem performative?
- Does their treatment of others align with how I want to be treated in a relationship?

The Importance of Kindness and Compassion in a Partner

A partner who consistently treats others with kindness and compassion is likely to bring those same qualities into your relationship. These traits foster trust, safety, and emotional intimacy, forming the foundation of a loving and respectful partnership. By observing how a potential partner treats others, singles can gain valuable insights into their character and decide whether their values align with their own vision for a healthy, lasting relationship.

Recognising Emotional Maturity in a Potential Partner

Emotional maturity is a vital quality in a healthy and lasting relationship. It encompasses self-awareness, the ability to manage emotions, effective communication, and a constructive approach to stress and conflict. For singles looking for a partner, identifying emotional maturity can help avoid toxic dynamics and build a strong, supportive connection. Here's how to recognise it:

Signs of Emotional Maturity

1. They Handle Stress Gracefully

What to Look For:

- Do they approach stressful situations with calmness and problem-solving, or do they lash out or shut down?
- Can they maintain perspective, focusing on solutions rather than getting stuck in blame or negativity?

Example: *If a project at work goes wrong, they acknowledge their feelings of frustration but take proactive steps to fix the issue instead of venting aimlessly or giving up.*

2. They Communicate Openly and Respectfully

What to Look For:

- Are they willing to express their feelings honestly without resorting to passive aggression, manipulation, or avoidance?

- Do they listen actively and seek to understand your perspective during discussions?

Example: *When upset about a miscommunication, they calmly explain how they feel and invite you to share your thoughts instead of stonewalling or attacking.*

3. They Take Responsibility for Their Actions

What to Look For:

- Do they own up to their mistakes without deflecting or making excuses?
- Are they willing to learn and grow from their experiences?

Example: *If they forget a commitment, they apologise sincerely and work to ensure it doesn't happen again, rather than becoming defensive or minimising the issue.*

4. They Manage Conflict Constructively

What to Look For:

- Do they focus on resolving the issue rather than "winning" the argument?

- Can they stay calm and respectful even when emotions are high?

***Example**: During a disagreement, they express their needs clearly, seek compromise, and avoid resorting to insults, shouting, or shutting down.*

5. They Regulate Their Emotions

What to Look For:

- Are they aware of their emotions and able to manage them without impulsive or destructive reactions?
- Do they practice patience and self-control, even in challenging situations?

***Example**: If they're running late and stuck in traffic, they acknowledge their frustration but remain composed instead of taking it out on others.*

6. They Show Empathy and Compassion

What to Look For:

- Can they put themselves in your shoes and validate your feelings?

- Do they approach others' struggles with kindness rather than judgment?

***Example**: If you've had a bad day, they offer support and understanding, even if they're tired or distracted.*

7. They Respect Boundaries

What to Look For:

- Do they honour your emotional, physical, and personal boundaries without pressuring or guilt-tripping you?
- Are they comfortable respectfully asserting their boundaries?

***Example**: If you ask for some alone time after a long day, they respect your request and give you space without making you feel guilty.*

8. They're Self-Aware

What to Look For:

- Are they aware of their strengths, weaknesses, and triggers?
- Do they actively work on improving themselves?

Example: *They recognise that they tend to be impatient and consciously practice mindfulness techniques to stay calm in stressful situations.*

Red Flags Indicating Emotional Immaturity

1. Frequent Overreactions:

They respond to minor issues with disproportionate anger or frustration.

2. Blaming Others:

They consistently shift responsibility for problems onto external factors or people.

3. Avoidance of Tough Conversations:

They evade discussions about feelings, conflicts, or future goals.

4. Inability to Apologise:

They refuse to admit fault or apologise sincerely, even when they've made a mistake.

5. Manipulative Behaviour:

They use guilt, passive-aggression, or other tactics to get their way.

Questions for Reflection

- How does this person typically handle setbacks or challenges?
- Are they able to express their emotions without becoming destructive or overwhelming?
- How do they approach disagreements—with a focus on resolving the issue or proving they're right?
- Do they respect your boundaries and communicate their own clearly?
- Do they demonstrate empathy and care, even in stressful or inconvenient situations?

Practical Advice

Observe Their Actions, Not Just Words

Look at how they behave in real-life situations. Words can be deceiving, but actions reflect true character.

Ask Open-Ended Questions

For example, "How do you typically handle stressful situations?" or "What do you think is the best way to resolve conflicts?" Their responses can reveal their level of emotional maturity.

Pay Attention to How They Treat Others

Their interactions with strangers, family, and friends can provide clues about their emotional regulation and empathy.

Be Patient

Emotional maturity develops over time. Focus on consistent patterns rather than isolated incidents.

Choosing a partner with emotional maturity lays the foundation for a resilient and supportive relationship. It ensures you can weather life's inevitable challenges together with mutual respect, understanding, and love.

Mutual Support and Encouragement: Building Each Other Up

Mutual support and encouragement are essential in healthy relationships, as they foster individual growth and strengthen the partnership. The right partner doesn't just celebrate your achievements; they also stand by you during challenges, helping you become the best version of yourself. For singles seeking the right partner, observing how someone supports and encourages their loved ones is a key indicator of compatibility and long-term relationship success.

Why Mutual Support Matters

1. Fosters Individual Growth:

Partners who encourage each other's dreams and ambitions help each other thrive personally and professionally.

2. Strengthens Emotional Intimacy:

Acts of encouragement deepen the bond, showing that each person is invested in the other's happiness and success.

3. Builds Resilience:

Facing life's challenges together with mutual support helps couples grow stronger, fostering trust and teamwork.

4. Creates a Shared Vision:

Supporting each other aligns the partnership with a common goal, even if individual aspirations differ.

Couples Who Support Each Other's Growth

A key component of a healthy relationship is that couples support and care for each other. They can do this by:

1. Building Confidence in New Ventures

A supportive partner doesn't just say "I believe in you" but actively participates in your journey, helping you overcome fears and practical challenges.

2. Supporting Each Other Through Career Transitions

Mutual support is a two-way street. A healthy relationship allows both partners to prioritise each other's ambitions at different times, fostering fairness and partnership.

3. Emotional Encouragement During Tough Times

A partner who offers emotional support during setbacks provides a safe space for vulnerability and healing, making it easier to face challenges together.

4. Encouraging Self-Care and Growth

Supporting personal growth isn't just about career goals; it's also about encouraging your partner to nurture themselves physically and emotionally.

5. Celebrating Each Other's Successes

True support is free of envy or competition. Instead, it's about being genuinely happy for your partner's achievements and celebrating their growth.

Red Flags to Watch For

Lack of Enthusiasm for Your Dreams:

If a partner is dismissive or indifferent about your goals, it may indicate they're not invested in your growth.

Undermining Your Efforts:

Subtle criticisms or discouragement can erode your confidence and indicate insecurity in the relationship.

One-Sided Support:

If support is consistently unbalanced, with one partner giving while the other takes, resentment may build over time.

Jealousy When You Are Successful and Progressive:

A partner who feels threatened by your achievements may struggle to celebrate your growth.

Questions to Reflect On

- Does this person encourage me to pursue my passions, even when it's inconvenient?
- How do they react to my successes—are they genuinely happy for me or dismissive?
- Have they supported others in their life, such as friends or family, in meaningful ways?
- Do I feel inspired and encouraged to grow when I'm with this person?

- Can I see myself doing the same for them?

A relationship rooted in mutual support and encouragement creates an environment where both partners feel valued and empowered to grow. When choosing a partner, look for someone who celebrates your wins, stands by you during tough times, and inspires you to reach your full potential. A supportive partner isn't just someone who loves you for who you are today—they're also excited to grow with you into the person you're becoming.

Healthy Communication: Techniques for Singles Seeking the Right Partner

Effective communication is the foundation of any strong and lasting relationship. It helps couples navigate differences, express needs, and build emotional intimacy. For singles looking for the right partner, practising and recognising healthy communication habits early on can set the tone for a successful partnership. Below are effective communication techniques and exercises to improve understanding, resolve conflicts, and strengthen connections.

Why Healthy Communication Matters

Builds Trust and Understanding:

Clear, honest conversations reduce misunderstandings and promote emotional intimacy.

Prevents Conflicts from Escalating:

Addressing issues calmly and constructively helps partners resolve disagreements before they grow.

Fosters Emotional Safety:

Healthy communication creates an environment where both partners feel heard, valued, and respected.

Sets the Tone for Long-Term Success:

How couples communicate during the early stages of a relationship often predicts long-term compatibility.

Key Techniques for Effective Communication

1. Use "I" Statements

What It Is: Instead of blaming or criticising your partner with "you" statements (e.g., "You never listen to me!"), express how you feel using "I" statements (e.g., "I feel unheard when I try to share my thoughts").

Why It Works: This technique reduces defensiveness and keeps the focus on your feelings and experiences, fostering constructive dialogue.

How to Practice:

Start with **"I feel..."** (emotion)

Add **"when you..."** (specific behaviour)

End with **"because..."** (impact on you)

Example: "I feel frustrated when plans change last minute because it disrupts my schedule."

2. Active Listening

What It Is: Actively focusing on your partner's words without interrupting, judging, or planning your response. It includes reflecting back what you heard to ensure understanding.

Why It Works: Active listening shows respect and validation, making the speaker feel heard and valued.

How to Practice:

- **Listen Without Interrupting**: Let your partner finish before responding.
- **Reflect**: Summarise what they said. For example: "It sounds like you're saying…"
- **Validate Feelings**: Acknowledge their emotions without judgment. Example: "I can understand why you'd feel that way."
- **Ask Clarifying Questions**: "Can you tell me more about what you mean?"

3. Nonverbal Communication Awareness

What It Is: Paying attention to body language, tone of voice, and facial expressions, which often convey more than words.

Why It Works: Nonverbal cues can enhance or contradict verbal communication. Being aware of these signals helps avoid misunderstandings.

How to Practice:

- Maintain eye contact to show engagement.
- Use open body language to signal receptivity.
- Watch for tension (crossed arms, clenched jaw) in your partner and address it gently.

4. The 10-Second Pause

What It Is: Pausing before responding, especially during heated discussions, to gather your thoughts and regulate emotions.

Why It Works: This helps prevent impulsive, hurtful reactions and encourages a more thoughtful response.

How to Practice:

When emotions run high, take a deep breath and count to ten before speaking.

Use the pause to consider: "What am I feeling, and what do I really want to say?"

5. Focus on Solutions, Not Blame

What It Is: Shifting the conversation from assigning fault to finding constructive ways to address the issue.

Why It Works: Solution-focused communication fosters teamwork and minimises defensiveness.

How to Practice:

Instead of saying, "You're always late," rather, say: "How can we manage our time better, so we're not rushed?"

Brainstorm solutions together and commit to actionable steps.

Communication Exercises

1. Reflective Listening Exercise

One person speaks for two minutes about a topic (e.g., their day or a challenge). The listener reflects what they heard without adding their opinion. Example: "You're saying that today was overwhelming because of back-to-back meetings."

Switch roles and repeat.

> ***Goal:***
> *Develop empathy and ensure both partners feel understood.*

2. The "Feelings Check-In"

Set aside time to share your feelings using "I" statements.

Each person takes a turn expressing how they've been feeling emotionally, physically, and mentally.

> ***Goal:***
> *Build a habit of sharing openly and staying attuned to each other's well-being.*

3. Shared Vision Exercise

Discuss questions like:

"What does a happy relationship look like to you?"

"What are your long-term goals, and how can I support them?"

Take turns listening actively and summarising each other's responses.

> ***Goal:***
> *Align values and goals while practising effective communication techniques.*

4. Practice Disagreeing Respectfully

Choose a low-stakes topic where you have different opinions (e.g., favourite movies or vacation spots).

Practice sharing your perspective calmly while actively listening to your partner's viewpoint.

> ***Goal:***
> *Build skills for handling disagreements without escalating tension.*

Red Flags of Unhealthy Communication

- Interrupting frequently or dismissing your opinions.
- Avoiding difficult conversations or "shutting down" emotionally.
- Using blame, criticism, or sarcasm during disagreements.
- Invalidating your feelings or making you feel small for expressing concerns.

Questions to Reflect On

- Does this person make me feel heard and valued when I express myself?
- Are they open to discussing challenges, or do they avoid difficult topics?
- Do they listen to understand, or just to respond?
- How do they handle disagreements—calmly or with hostility?
- Do I feel safe and respected communicating my needs to them?

Healthy communication is a cornerstone of successful relationships. By using techniques like "I" statements, active listening, and focusing on solutions, you can foster stronger connections and assess whether a potential partner shares these skills. Observing how someone communicates under both positive and challenging circumstances offers invaluable insight into their compatibility as a lifelong partner.

Common Interests: The Importance of Common Interests in Choosing the Right Partner

While opposites can sometimes attract, common interests play a significant role in fostering connection, companionship, and long-term satisfaction in a relationship. Shared hobbies and activities provide opportunities for bonding, creating memories, and maintaining a sense of fun and excitement throughout the partnership. When seeking the right partner, evaluating whether you share meaningful interests can help you identify compatibility and envision a fulfilling future together.

Why Common Interests Matter

1. Building Emotional Connection

Shared hobbies and activities offer a natural way to connect emotionally.

Engaging in activities together fosters teamwork, shared laughter, and mutual appreciation.

2. Creating Quality Time

Relationships thrive on spending meaningful time together. Common interests ensure that both partners can enjoy shared experiences without feeling forced or compromising too much on preferences.

3. Strengthening Compatibility

While differences add variety, having common interests helps align lifestyles and priorities.

It minimises friction over how to spend free time and allows both partners to feel fulfilled.

4. Supporting Growth and Learning

Exploring hobbies together encourages personal growth and learning new skills as a team.

It helps maintain the relationship's excitement and novelty as you discover new activities.

The Value of Shared Hobbies and Activities

Building a Sense of Partnership

Example: A couple who loves travelling the world, working together to planning the countries they should go to and sharing the satisfaction of reaching a destination country.

Value: This reinforces the idea of being "on the same team," creating a strong sense of partnership.

Nurturing Long-Term Compatibility

Example: Partners who enjoy cooking together can turn mealtimes into bonding moments, while those who share a love for music might attend concerts or create playlists together.

Value: These shared activities become traditions that deepen the relationship over time.

Providing a Shared Social Circle

Example: Joining a local sports league, book club, or dance class as a couple can expand your social network with like-minded individuals.

Value: A shared community enhances the relationship by offering additional avenues for connection and fun.

Balancing Individual and Shared Interests

While common interests are vital, maintaining individual hobbies ensures each partner has personal space and independence. A healthy balance prevents burnout and keeps the relationship dynamic.

How to Explore Common Interests While Dating

Ask Questions Early On

Examples:

"What do you enjoy doing in your free time?"

"What's a hobby you've always wanted to try?"

This reveals whether your interests align and gives clues about your compatibility.

Try New Things Together

Dating is a great opportunity to experiment with hobbies and explore new activities.

It shows how willing both partners are to step out of their comfort zones and enjoy shared experiences.

Reflect on Natural Compatibility

Ask yourself: Do we gravitate toward similar activities without much effort?

Example: If one partner loves attending parties while the other prefers quiet weekends at home, consider how to balance these differences.

Real-Life Stories of Shared Interests in Relationships

Strengthening a Relationship Through Adventure

Story: Anna and Liam bonded over their love for travel during their first few dates. They began planning trips together, exploring new cultures, and making memories. Their shared passion for adventure became the backbone of their relationship, giving them a joint goal of visiting every continent together.

Takeaway: Shared interests like travel create a sense of excitement and give partners a shared vision to pursue.

Growing Closer Through Creativity

Story: E and J discovered a mutual love for painting during a casual date. They began setting up painting nights at home, experimenting with styles and encouraging each other's creativity. This hobby helped them relax and express themselves in new ways.

Takeaway: Creative hobbies can bring couples closer by allowing them to learn and grow together.

Tips to Identify and Build Common Interests

Be Honest About Your Interests

Share your genuine hobbies and passions upfront. This helps attract someone who values the same things.

Explore New Activities

Be open to trying out your potential partner's interests and inviting them to explore yours. This builds mutual respect and understanding.

Look for Patterns in Conversations

Pay attention to what topics excite them. If they frequently mention outdoor activities, art, or sports, it may be a shared area of interest to explore.

Find Shared Values Within Interests

Does the activity reflect the values you share? For example, volunteering together might indicate a shared sense of compassion or community involvement.

Questions for Reflection

- What hobbies or activities are non-negotiable for me in a relationship?
- Am I willing to try new things and step outside my comfort zone for a partner?
- How do I feel about balancing shared interests with individual pursuits?
- Do our lifestyles naturally align, or will we need to adjust to spend time together?

Common interests provide the glue that helps couples stay connected and enjoy each other's company over the long term. Seeking a partner, finding someone who shares your hobbies and values makes it easier to build a fulfilling relationship. While differences can add excitement, a strong foundation of shared activities ensures that your time together is meaningful, fun, and enriching.

Physical and Emotional Attraction: Balancing Both with God's Perspective

When seeking the right partner, physical attraction is often the initial spark, but emotional attraction—rooted in shared values, trust, and vulnerability—provides the foundation for a God-honouring and fulfilling relationship. From a Biblical perspective, both aspects can play a role, but emotional safety and spiritual alignment should always take precedence. Recognising God's design for relationships ensures that both physical and emotional attraction are viewed healthily and purposefully.

God's Perspective on Attraction

Physical Attraction is Part of God's Design

God created humans to appreciate beauty and be drawn to one another physically. In Song of Solomon, the physical and romantic attraction between the lovers is celebrated as a gift from God.

> *"You are altogether beautiful, my love; there is no flaw in you." (Song of Solomon 4:7)*

However, physical attraction is never meant to outweigh the importance of inner character and spiritual maturity.

Emotional and Spiritual Connection Reflect God's Heart

Scripture emphasises the importance of the heart and character over outward appearance:

> *"Man looks at the outward appearance, but the Lord looks at the heart." (1 Samuel 16:7)*

A deeply emotional and spiritual bond rooted in shared faith and values honours God's purpose for relationships and mirrors Christ's selfless love for the church.

Emotional Safety Reflects God's Love

In a healthy relationship, emotional safety allows both partners to express themselves openly, mirroring the trust and grace God extends to us:

> *"Above all, love each other deeply, because love covers over a multitude of sins."* (1 Peter 4:8)

Why Both Physical and Emotional Attraction Matter

1. Physical Attraction is an Entry Point

Physical attraction can ignite interest and curiosity about a person, and there's nothing wrong with acknowledging this natural aspect of relationships.

However, physical attraction alone cannot sustain a relationship if deeper emotional and spiritual bonds are lacking.

2. Emotional Attraction Anchors the Relationship

Emotional attraction grows through shared values, vulnerability, and mutual respect. It is this connection that helps couples weather challenges and find joy in the mundane.

Proverbs 31:30 reminds us that true beauty lies beyond the surface:

> *"Charm is deceptive, and beauty is fleeting; but a woman who fears the Lord is to be praised."*

3. Emotional Safety Mirrors God's Design

Feeling emotionally safe in a relationship reflects God's intention for love: one rooted in grace, patience, and kindness (1 Corinthians 13:4-7).

A relationship where both partners feel safe being vulnerable fosters trust and a Christ-centred connection.

Encouraging Singles to Explore Both Aspects

1. Seek God's Guidance in Assessing Attraction

Pray for wisdom to discern whether a relationship balances physical and emotional attraction in a God-honouring way:

> *"If any of you lacks wisdom, you should ask God, who gives generously to all without finding fault."* (James 1:5)

Reflect: Does this relationship glorify God and align with His purpose for your life?

2. Don't Prioritise Physical Attraction Over Character

While physical attraction is important, consider whether your partner exhibits the fruit of the Spirit (Galatians 5:22-23) such as love, joy, peace, patience, and kindness.

Ask: Does their inner character inspire you to grow closer to God?

3. Cultivate Emotional Safety Through Christ-Centred Values

Emotional safety thrives when both partners are anchored in Christ's love and humility.

Build the relationship on a foundation of shared faith, regular prayer, and open, honest communication.

How to Foster Emotional Safety in a God-Honouring Way

1. Build on Mutual Respect

Treat each other with dignity, reflecting Christ's command to love as He loved us:

> *"Do to others as you would have them do to you." (Luke 6:31)*

2. Pray Together

Incorporate prayer into your relationship to invite God's presence and guidance.

Example: Pray for clarity, patience, and alignment in your relationship's direction.

3. Handle Conflict with Grace

Emotional safety means navigating disagreements in a way that honours God, with patience and forgiveness:

> *"Be completely humble and gentle; be patient, bearing with one another in love." (Ephesians 4:2)*

4. Surround Yourself with Godly Counsel

Seek advice from trusted mentors or spiritual leaders to ensure the relationship aligns with God's principles:

> *"Plans fail for lack of counsel, but with many advisers they succeed." (Proverbs 15:22)*

Stories Illustrating God's Perspective on Attraction

Prioritising Emotional Safety Over Appearance

Story:

M initially dated someone she found physically attractive but realised he wasn't supportive of her faith journey. Later, she met A, whose kindness, humility, and love for God drew her in. Over time, M found herself deeply emotionally and spiritually attracted to him, realising that emotional safety and shared faith brought a deeper joy than physical attraction alone.

> ***Takeaway***: *Emotional and spiritual connection that aligns with God's plan sustains a relationship far more than surface-level attraction.*

A Christ-Centred Balance

Story:

D and G were both drawn to each other's outward appearance, but what cemented their relationship was their shared love for ministry and prayer. They made a habit of serving together, and their bond grew as they saw each other's faith in action. G described feeling safe with D because he reflected Christ's selfless love in both word and deed.

> ***Takeaway***: *Physical attraction is a blessing, but emotional safety and shared spiritual purpose bring lasting fulfillment.*

Questions to Reflect On:

Physical Attraction

- Am I focusing solely on outward appearance, or do I also value their spiritual maturity and inner qualities?
- Does this person honour God in their words, actions, and how they treat me?

Emotional Attraction

- Do I feel safe sharing my thoughts and vulnerabilities with this person?
- Are we both committed to putting God at the centre of our relationship?

Practical Tips for Balancing Both

1. Pray for Clarity and Discernment

Ask God to help you balance physical attraction with a deeper desire for emotional and spiritual compatibility.

2. Engage in God-Honouring Activities

Spend time together in ways that encourage spiritual growth, such as attending church, volunteering, or participating in Bible studies.

3. Focus on Emotional Safety as a Priority

Evaluate whether your partner's behaviour reflects Christlike qualities. Emotional safety comes from mutual respect, patience, and humility.

4. Wait for God's Timing

Don't rush into a relationship based solely on physical attraction. Trust God to guide you to someone who will fulfil both your emotional and spiritual needs.

Physical and emotional attraction both play roles in God's design for relationships, but emotional safety, rooted in shared faith and Christlike love, is paramount. By seeking God's guidance, prioritising spiritual maturity, and cultivating emotional connection, singles can find a partner who brings both joy and a Christ-centred foundation for a thriving relationship.

Family and Relationship Background: Guidance for Discussing Family Backgrounds and Past Relationships

Seeking the right partner and discussing family backgrounds and past relationships is an important step in fostering transparency, understanding, and trust. These conversations, when approached thoughtfully and prayerfully, can strengthen emotional and spiritual connection. They also provide insights into each other's values, character, and healing journeys. The Bible offers timeless principles that guide us in engaging these discussions with wisdom and grace.

Why These Conversations Matter

Understanding Influences

Family backgrounds shape our values, communication styles, and expectations in relationships. Exploring this provides clarity about each partner's experiences and how they might impact the future.

> *Proverbs 22:6: "Train up a child in the way he should go; even when he is old he will not depart from it." This verse reminds us that family influences can have lasting effects.*

Building Trust Through Transparency

Discussing past relationships, when done with discretion, demonstrates honesty and openness. It sets a foundation of trust essential for a strong partnership.

> *Ephesians 4:25: "Therefore each of you must put off falsehood and speak truthfully to your neighbor, for we are all members of one body."*

Identifying Potential Challenges

Conversations about family dynamics or past wounds help identify potential areas of growth or healing. This promotes mutual support and deeper connection.

> *Galatians 6:2: "Carry each other's burdens, and in this way you will fulfill the law of Christ."*

How to Approach the Conversation

Pray for Wisdom

Before delving into these topics, pray for discernment, humility, and the right words to share.

> *James 1:5: "If any of you lacks wisdom, you should ask God, who gives generously to all without finding fault, and it will be given to you."*

Choose the Right Time and Setting

These sensitive conversations require a setting that allows for privacy and focused attention. Avoid rushing into them; allow the relationship to grow naturally first.

Be Honest Yet Respectful

Share your story with honesty but avoid oversharing or speaking negatively about others. Respect your own and the other person's boundaries.

Listen with Empathy

Approach your partner's sharing with a nonjudgmental attitude. Acknowledge their experiences and affirm their courage in sharing.

Focus on Growth and Redemption

Frame discussions around how you've grown or sought healing, emphasising God's transformative work in your life.

> *2 Corinthians 5:17: "Therefore, if anyone is in Christ, the new creation has come: The old has gone, the new is here!"*

Key Questions for Discussion

Family Background

- How has your family shaped your views on relationships, marriage, and parenting?
- What family traditions or values are important to you?
- Are there family dynamics that might impact our relationship? (e.g., unresolved conflicts, cultural expectations)
- How do you handle family conflicts or differing opinions?

Past Relationships

- What have you learned from previous relationships about yourself and what you're looking for in a partner?
- How has God used past experiences to prepare you for a future relationship?
- Are there any unresolved wounds or areas where you're seeking healing?
- What boundaries do you think are important to establish based on your past experiences?

Biblical Encouragement for Vulnerability and Healing

Forgiveness and Healing

Past wounds should not define the future, but forgiveness and healing are essential for moving forward.

> *Colossians 3:13: "Bear with each other and forgive one another if any of you has a grievance against someone. Forgive as the Lord forgave you."*

God's Redemption in Brokenness

Sharing past mistakes or pain can highlight God's grace and redemptive power.

> *Joel 2:25: "I will repay you for the years the locusts have eaten."*

Mutual Accountability

Couples should support each other in pursuing healing and honouring God in their relationship.

> *Proverbs 27:17: "As iron sharpens iron, so one person sharpens another."*

Things to Avoid

Judgment or Criticism

Criticising your partner's family or past experiences can breed resentment. Instead, approach with understanding.

Unnecessary Details

Avoid sharing graphic or unnecessary details about past relationships. Focus on lessons learned and growth instead of rehashing painful specifics.

Comparisons

Refrain from comparing your partner to past relationships or family members. This can erode their confidence and trust.

Discussing family backgrounds and past relationships is an important step for singles seeking a Christ-centred partnership. When approached prayerfully, these conversations foster trust, understanding, and growth. By relying on Biblical principles and prioritising mutual respect, couples can navigate these discussions with grace, laying the groundwork for a strong and God-honouring relationship.

Reflection Questions:

- How can I show empathy and understanding when discussing sensitive topics?
- Am I prepared to share my story in a way that glorifies God and reflects my growth?
- How will my faith guide me in navigating any challenges revealed in these conversations?

Vision for the Future:

Here are practical exercises to help singles articulate their long-term goals and align their future vision with a potential partner. These exercises encourage prayerful reflection, honest conversations, and shared dreams about the future, grounded in biblical principles.

1. Life Map Exercise

Purpose: Reflect on personal experiences, define core values, and envision the future.

How to Do It:

1. Divide your life into three phases: past, present, and future.
2. Write down key milestones (e.g., spiritual growth, career, relationships).
3. Reflect on lessons learned and how they shape your future goals.
4. Share your life map with your partner and discuss how your visions align.

Key Bible Verse:

> *"For I know the plans I have for you," declares the Lord, "plans to prosper you and not to harm you, plans to give you hope and a future." – Jeremiah 29:11*

Reflection Questions:

- How has God shaped your journey so far?
- What key experiences influence your vision for the future?

2. Shared Vision Board

Purpose: Visualise and discuss shared priorities and goals.

How to Do It:

1. Gather materials (e.g., magazines, markers, or digital tools).
2. Individually, create a collage representing your dreams for the future (e.g., marriage, family, ministry, career).

3. Present your vision boards to each other, explaining your choices.
4. Combine overlapping goals into a shared vision board.

Key Bible Verse:

> *"Write the vision; make it plain on tablets, so he may run who reads it." – Habakkuk 2:2*

Reflection Questions:

- What themes do you both prioritise (e.g., faith, community, family)?
- Are there areas where your visions differ, and how can you reconcile them?

3. The "10-Year Letter" Exercise

Purpose: Articulate long-term aspirations and create a roadmap for the future.

How to Do It:

1. Write a letter to yourself describing your life 10 years from now.

2. Include details about spiritual growth, career, relationships, family, and community involvement.
3. Share your letters with each other and discuss how to support one another's goals.

Key Bible Verse:

"Commit to the Lord whatever you do, and he will establish your plans." – Proverbs 16:3

Reflection Questions:

- What role does faith play in shaping your long-term vision?
- How can you align your aspirations with a shared future?

4. The Pillars of Purpose Exercise

Purpose: Identify core priorities that will guide your life together.

How to Do It:

1. Reflect individually on what matters most (e.g., faith, family, service, career).

2. Share your lists and categorise them into "non-negotiables" and "flexible priorities."
3. Create a joint mission statement that captures your shared purpose.

Key Bible Verse:

> *"Unless the Lord builds the house, the builders labor in vain." – Psalm 127:1*

Reflection Questions:

- What core values are non-negotiable for your future?
- How will your shared purpose reflect your faith and glorify God?

5. Prayer and Goal-Setting

Purpose: Seek God's guidance in shaping your future together.

How to Do It:

1. Dedicate a time to pray together about your individual and shared futures.

2. List specific goals for different areas of life (e.g., spiritual growth, family, finances).
3. Ask each other reflective questions to ensure alignment (e.g., How will we prioritise our faith? What are our financial goals?).
4. Revisit and adjust your goals periodically.

Key Bible Verse:

> *"In their hearts humans plan their course, but the Lord establishes their steps." – Proverbs 16:9*

Reflection Questions:

- What specific steps can you take to pursue God's vision for your relationship?
- How will you stay accountable to one another in pursuing these goals?

6. The "What If" Game

Purpose: Explore hypothetical scenarios to clarify values and priorities.

How to Do It:

1. Take turns posing "What if" questions about the future (e.g., What if we're called to move for ministry? What if we face financial challenges?).
2. Discuss how you would handle these scenarios together, grounding your answers in faith.

Key Bible Verse:

"Two are better than one, because they have a good return for their labor: If either of them falls down, one can help the other up." – Ecclesiastes 4:9-10

Reflection Questions:

- How do you handle uncertainty and change?
- How can you work together to overcome challenges while remaining faithful to God?

7. Strengths and Growth Chart

Purpose: Understand each other's strengths and areas for growth to create a balanced partnership.

How to Do It:

1. List your strengths and areas where you need support.
2. Share your lists and discuss how your strengths can complement each other.
3. Set goals to grow together spiritually, emotionally, and practically.

Key Bible Verse:

> *"Each of you should use whatever gift you have received to serve others, as faithful stewards of God's grace in its various forms." – 1 Peter 4:10*

Reflection Questions:

- How can your strengths support one another's long-term goals?
- What steps can you take to grow together in areas where you feel weak?

These exercises create opportunities for you to articulate and align your long-term goals with a potential partner while inviting God into the process. By praying, reflecting, and discussing openly, you can build a shared vision that honours your faith and sets a strong foundation for the future.

Final Reflection Question: How can you ensure that your vision for the future reflects God's will for your life and your relationship?

4

The Role of Community and Mentorship

The Role of a Supportive Faith Community in Encouragement and Accountability

No one should make life-altering decisions alone. This chapter emphasises the importance of seeking wise counsel from trusted mentors, family members, and spiritual leaders. Surrounding yourself with a strong faith community can provide guidance and insight into the potential of a relationship.

Story Segment: Sarah, in her quest for a godly partner, started attending a small group at her church. There, she met a married couple who became her mentors. They had been through ups and downs in their marriage and were able to offer Sarah advice on what to look for in a relationship and how to recognise red flags. This community became a source of encouragement and accountability for Sarah.

The chapter stresses the importance of listening to people who have walked the path before and allowing them to speak into your life, especially when emotions might cloud judgment.

Being part of a supportive faith community offers a unique environment for spiritual growth, encouragement, and accountability. Hebrews 10:24-25 reminds believers of the value of fellowship:

> *"And let us consider how we may spur one another on toward love and good deeds, not giving up meeting together, as some are in the habit of doing, but encouraging one another – and all the more as you see the Day approaching."*

This passage underscores the importance of gathering with other believers to strengthen one another in faith, motivate acts of love and service, and remain steadfast in Christian living.

Benefits of a Supportive Faith Community

Encouragement in Life's Challenges

A faith community offers emotional and spiritual support during difficulties. Members can pray for one another, provide comfort, and share wisdom grounded in Scripture.

***Example**: When struggling with a job loss, being surrounded by believers who offer encouragement, practical help, and prayer can renew hope and trust in God.*

Accountability in Spiritual Growth

Fellow believers can lovingly hold each other accountable for maintaining a Christ-centred life, reminding each other of their commitments and encouraging repentance when needed.

Example: *A trusted friend from church gently points out when someone is neglecting prayer or straying from Biblical values, helping them realign with God's will.*

Opportunities to Serve and Grow

By engaging in service within the church, individuals not only contribute to the community but also grow in their faith. Working together for a common purpose strengthens bonds and deepens spiritual maturity.

Example: *Volunteering at a food drive or mentoring younger believers allows individuals to live out their faith actively.*

Fostering a Sense of Belonging

A church community provides a safe, accepting environment where individuals feel valued and connected.

This sense of belonging reinforces faith and combats loneliness.

Example: *Being part of a small group creates opportunities to share life's highs and lows with people who genuinely care.*

A supportive faith community, as described in Hebrews 10:24-25, is essential for thriving spiritually. By staying connected, believers can encourage one another to persevere in faith, grow in love, and remain accountable in their walk with Christ. Whether through small groups, volunteer work, or fellowship, engaging actively with your church deepens both personal faith and the collective strength of the community.

Seeking Wisdom: The Importance of Mentorship for Singles Before Entering Relationships

Mentorship is a vital resource for singles preparing for relationships, offering wisdom, guidance, and encouragement to build a strong foundation for future partnerships. By learning from those with experience and insight, singles can better understand themselves, cultivate healthy relationship skills, and avoid common pitfalls.

Why Mentorship is Essential

Provides Wisdom and Perspective

Mentors, especially those who have navigated relationships successfully, can offer valuable insights that help singles recognise what matters most in a relationship.

Example: A mentor might share how prioritising shared values helped them navigate challenges with their spouse, emphasising what contributes to lasting love.

Helps Identify Blind Spots

Trusted mentors can gently point out areas for personal growth, such as emotional maturity, communication habits, or unrealistic expectations.

Example: A mentor could guide someone to address a pattern of avoiding conflict, which might hinder relationship success.

Models Healthy Relationships

Observing mentors or couples who demonstrate respect, love, and effective conflict resolution provides singles with a tangible example of what a healthy relationship looks like.

Example: A couple may share how they maintain open communication or balance personal goals with shared priorities.

Encourages Emotional and Spiritual Preparation

Mentorship helps singles focus on becoming the best version of themselves before seeking a partner, fostering emotional health, and deepening their relationship with God.

Example: A mentor might encourage journaling, prayer, or counselling to work through personal issues before dating.

Reduces Pressure and Isolation

Seeking mentorship can ease the pressure to "figure it out alone" and provide reassurance that others have faced similar challenges.

Example: A single person feeling anxious about dating can find encouragement from a mentor who shares how they overcame similar struggles.

Encouraging Singles to Seek Mentorship

Choose the Right Mentors

Seek guidance from individuals who embody the qualities you admire, such as integrity, emotional intelligence, and faithfulness.

Look for couples who demonstrate love, respect, and a commitment to shared values.

Be Open and Honest

Share your questions, fears, and experiences honestly to gain meaningful feedback.

Be receptive to constructive criticism and advice, even when it challenges you.

Engage in Consistent Meetings

Commit to regular check-ins with a mentor or small group to build trust and ensure accountability.

Example: Monthly coffee meetups or joining a Bible study led by a mentor couple.

Learn Through Observation

Observe how mentors navigate everyday interactions, resolve conflicts, and support each other.

Example: Spend time with a couple to see how they handle decisions like budgeting or parenting.

Ask Specific Questions

Gain clarity by asking mentors targeted questions about relationships, such as:

- How did you navigate challenges early in your relationship?
- What qualities should I prioritise in a partner?
- How do you keep God at the centre of your marriage?

Practical Steps to Find Mentors

Within Your Church:

Join small groups, volunteer, or attend workshops where you can connect with potential mentors.

Ask a pastor or church leader to recommend experienced couples who might be open to mentoring.

Family and Friends:

Look for relatives or friends whose relationships inspire you and ask if they're willing to share their wisdom.

Community Resources:

Many churches and organisations offer pre-marital or singles-focused mentorship programs.

Mentorship equips you with the tools and wisdom needed to enter relationships with confidence and clarity. By seeking advice from trusted mentors or observing healthy relationships, you can learn to prioritise character, communicate effectively, and establish realistic expectations. Embracing mentorship is not a sign of weakness; it is a proactive step toward building strong, God-honouring relationships.

Key Scripture for Reflection

> *"Plans fail for lack of counsel, but with many advisers they succeed." – Proverbs 15:22*

Accountability: The Need for Accountability Partners

Accountability partners are trusted individuals who provide encouragement, guidance, and support to help singles stay aligned with their values, goals, and spiritual walk. For singles, this support system is especially important in navigating relationships, personal growth, and the challenges of daily life.

An accountability partner offers:

Encouragement:

They motivate you to pursue personal and spiritual growth.

Perspective:

They help you make wise decisions by offering objective advice.

Support:

They are there during moments of struggle or temptation to steer you back on course.

Why Accountability Matters

Maintains Focus on Godly Living

Singles often face societal pressures and temptations that can lead them away from their values. Accountability partners provide reminders to prioritise faith and live in a way that honours God.

Example: An accountability partner can encourage you to remain patient during seasons of singleness, trusting God's timing.

Helps Establish Boundaries

Whether in dating relationships, friendships, or personal habits, accountability partners can help ensure healthy boundaries are respected.

Example: If you're dating, your partner can check in with you about maintaining physical and emotional boundaries.

Encourages Wise Decision-Making

Singles often make significant life decisions, such as career changes, moving, or choosing a partner. Accountability partners can provide counsel to ensure choices align with long-term goals and faith.

Example: Before entering a new relationship, they might ask questions about compatibility and shared values.

Provides a Safe Space for Vulnerability

Singles benefit from a trusted confidant who listens without judgment and offers constructive feedback, helping them grow emotionally and spiritually.

Example: When struggling with loneliness, an accountability partner can provide support and redirect focus toward God's promises.

How to Establish an Accountability Support System

1. Identify the Right Person

Look for someone who is:

- Spiritually mature and committed to their growth.
- Trustworthy and able to keep conversations confidential.
- Willing to provide honest, constructive feedback.
- Empathetic and supportive.

***Tip**: Consider a mentor, a mature friend, or a member of your church community.*

2. Clarify Expectations

Discuss the purpose and boundaries of your accountability relationship. Be clear about:

- The areas where you need support (e.g., purity, decision-making, faith consistency).
- How often you will meet or check in (weekly, bi-weekly, etc.)?

- The level of honesty and vulnerability expected.

***Example**: Agree that you'll ask each other tough questions or pray together regularly.*

Use Technology to Stay Connected

If meeting in person isn't always possible, leverage technology for accountability.

Suggestions: Use video calls, messaging apps, or accountability software to stay in touch.

***Example**: Apps like Covenant Eyes can help singles maintain purity in online activities, with regular reports shared with their accountability partner.*

Join a Small Group or Bible Study

Small groups provide a natural environment for building accountability relationships with like-minded individuals.

How to Start: Look for groups focused on singles or young adults within your church.

Be Vulnerable and Honest

Open communication is essential for accountability to work. Share your struggles, temptations, and goals openly.

Tip: Remember that accountability partners are there to support, not judge, you.

Make It Reciprocal

If possible, form a mutual accountability partnership where you also support the other person's growth.

***Example**: Pray for each other, share Scripture, and celebrate each other's victories.*

Topics for Accountability Conversations

Faith Practices: Are you consistent in prayer, Bible study, and attending church?

Relationships: Are you maintaining boundaries in dating? Are you pursuing relationships that honour God?

Personal Growth: Are you working toward goals and habits that align with your values?

Struggles: Are you addressing areas of temptation or weakness constructively?

Reflection Questions

- Who in my life could help me grow spiritually and personally through accountability?
- Am I willing to be open and honest with someone about my challenges and goals?
- How can I prioritise regular check-ins with an accountability partner?

Accountability partners are vital for singles who want to stay rooted in their faith and make wise, value-driven choices. By surrounding yourself with supportive, honest individuals who genuinely care about your growth, you'll find the strength to navigate life's challenges and remain faithful to God's purpose for your life.

Key Scripture for Reflection

"As iron sharpens iron, so one person sharpens another."
– Proverbs 27:17

5
The Power of Prayer and Discernment

Prayer is a vital part of seeking God's will in any area of life, especially in relationships. This chapter dives deep into how to pray for discernment and clarity when choosing a partner.

It provides specific prayers for wisdom, patience, and the ability to hear God's voice amidst all the noise.

Key Lessons:

Patience in Prayer: Waiting on God's timing is difficult, but it's essential. Rushing into relationships out of impatience can lead to heartbreak.

Recognising God's Voice: Sometimes, what we want isn't what God has planned for us. This chapter helps readers discern when God is opening doors and when He's closing them.

Story Segment: After months of prayer, Sarah began dating someone from her church. He seemed to meet all the criteria: kind, thoughtful, and deeply involved in ministry. But something felt off. She couldn't explain it, so she prayed fervently for clarity. Through prayer, Sarah realised that while this man was a good person, he wasn't God's choice for her. The peace she sought never came, and eventually, she ended the relationship, trusting that God had someone better in mind.

The Importance of Prayer In Seeking A Life Partner:

Prayers for a life partner are a powerful way for singles to invite God into their search for love and companionship. Through prayer, we can seek guidance, clarity, and wisdom, aligning our desires with God's will for our lives. The Bible assures us of God's care and provision, encouraging us to trust Him in every area of our lives, including relationships.

The Power of Prayer for Life Partners

1. Aligns Desires with God's Will:

Prayer invites God to shape our hearts and desires according to His perfect plan. Jeremiah 29:11 reminds us, *"For I know the plans I have for you," declares the Lord, "plans to prosper you and not to harm you, plans to give you hope and a future."*

2. Provides Peace and Clarity:

In moments of uncertainty or emotional turmoil, prayer can bring peace and help us discern God's direction. Philippians 4:6-7 encourages us, *"Do not be anxious about anything, but in every situation, by prayer and petition, with thanksgiving, present your requests to God. And the peace of God, which transcends all understanding, will guard your hearts and your minds in Christ Jesus."*

3. Builds Patience and Trust:

Waiting on God requires patience, and prayer is a way to cultivate trust in His timing. Psalm 37:4-5 states, *"Take delight in the Lord, and he will give you the desires of your heart. Commit your way to the Lord; trust in him and he will do this."*

Prayers for Guidance, Clarity, and Wisdom

1. A Prayer for Guidance

Heavenly Father, I come before You with an open heart, seeking Your guidance in finding a life partner. You know the desires of my heart and the plans You have for me. Please lead me to someone who will help me grow closer to You and fulfill Your purpose for our lives together. Teach me to trust in Your timing and remain faithful in prayer. In Jesus' name, Amen.

> ***Key Verse:*** *"The heart of man plans his way, but the Lord establishes his steps." – Proverbs 16:9*

2. A Prayer for Clarity

Lord, I ask for clarity as I navigate relationships. Help me to recognise the qualities and character traits that align with Your Word. Remove any confusion or distractions that may lead me astray. Give me wisdom to make choices that honor You and to see clearly the path You have set before me. Thank You for being the light in my journey. Amen.

> ***Key Verse:*** *"Your word is a lamp to my feet and a light to my path." – Psalm 119:105*

3. A Prayer for Wisdom

Dear God, grant me wisdom as I seek a life partner. Help me discern the difference between what I want and what I need. Teach me to listen to Your voice and make decisions based on Your will. Let Your wisdom guide my thoughts, words, and actions, that I may reflect Your love and grace in my relationships. In Jesus' name, Amen.

> ***Key Verse:*** *"If any of you lacks wisdom, you should ask God, who gives generously to all without finding fault, and it will be given to you." – James 1:5*

Prayers to Understand God's Will

1. A Prayer of Surrender

Father, I surrender my desires and plans for a life partner to You. Let Your will be done in my life, not mine. Shape my heart to seek Your kingdom first, trusting that You will provide all I need. Tha nk You for loving me and preparing a good future for me. Help me to rest in Your promises. Amen.

> ***Key Verse:*** *"But seek first his kingdom and his righteousness, and all these things will be given to you as well." – Matthew 6:33*

2. A Prayer for Patience and Trust

Lord, I confess that waiting can be hard, but I choose to trust in Your perfect timing. Help me to grow in patience and faith as I wait for the partner You have chosen for me. Keep me rooted in Your Word, and may I find joy in Your presence during this season of waiting. Thank You for Your unfailing love. Amen.

> ***Key Verse:*** *"Wait for the Lord; be strong, and let your heart take courage; wait for the Lord!"* – **Psalm 27:14**

As you pray for a life partner, remember to trust God's sovereignty and timing. He knows your heart, your desires, and the plans He has for you. Stay steadfast in faith, commit your desires to Him, and let His peace guard your heart. Trust that God's best is worth the wait!

Recognising God's Voice: Discerning God's Leading Through Prayer and Meditation

Discerning God's leading requires a deep relationship with Him, cultivated through prayer, meditation, and attentiveness to His Word. Proverbs 3:5-6 assures us, *"Trust in the Lord with all your heart and lean not on your own understanding; in all your ways submit to him, and he will make your paths straight."* By surrendering our desires and listening for His guidance, we can align our decisions with His will.

Steps to Discern God's Leading

1. Trust and Surrender

Fully trusting God means letting go of personal agendas and fears. Surrender your desires for a life partner to Him, believing that His plans are better than your own. Trust is the foundation for hearing His voice.

2. Commit to Daily Prayer

Prayer opens the line of communication with God. Talk to Him honestly about your thoughts, feelings, and uncertainties. Ask for His wisdom and guidance in all decisions.

3. Meditate on God's Word

The Bible is the primary way God speaks to us. Reflect on passages related to His guidance, promises, and love. Psalm 119:105 says, *"Your word is a lamp to my feet and a light to my path."* Allow Scripture to shape your perspective.

4. Listen in Silence

God often speaks in stillness. After praying, take time to sit quietly in His presence. Resist the urge to rush or fill the silence with distractions. Remember Elijah's experience in 1 Kings 19:12, where God spoke in a gentle whisper rather than through loud, dramatic means.

5. Seek Confirmation

God's guidance is consistent with His Word, His character, and the counsel of godly mentors. If you sense God leading you in a certain direction, seek confirmation through

Scripture, prayer, and advice from spiritually mature individuals.

6. Pay Attention to Peace

God's guidance is often accompanied by an inner sense of peace, even if the decision requires faith. Colossians 3:15 reminds us, *"Let the peace of Christ rule in your hearts."*

Techniques for Quieting the Mind

Find a Quiet Space:

Choose a place free from distractions. This could be a room in your home, a garden, or a church.

Practice Deep Breathing:

Breathe deeply and slowly to calm your mind and body. Focus on each breath, releasing tension and centering your thoughts on God.

Focus on a Scripture or Phrase:

Meditate on a short verse like Proverbs 3:5-6 or a phrase such as, *"Speak, Lord, for your servant is listening"* (1 Samuel 3:10). Repeat it silently as you reflect.

Journal Your Thoughts:

Write down your prayers, thoughts, and impressions during your quiet time. This helps clarify what God may be speaking to your heart.

Start Small:

Begin with just five minutes of silence and gradually increase the time as you grow more comfortable with stillness.

Use Worship Music:

Soft, instrumental worship music can help set a prayerful atmosphere and focus your mind on God.

Listening for God's Guidance

Ask Open-Ended Questions:

Pray, "Lord, what do You want me to know about this decision?" or "How should I proceed in this season?"

Be Patient:

Answers may not come immediately. Trust that God speaks in His timing, often revealing His plans step by step.

Reflect on Impressions:

Pay attention to recurring thoughts, ideas, or Scriptures that come to mind during prayer. They might be God's way of communicating.

Stay Consistent:

Regular times of prayer and meditation help train your spirit to recognise God's voice more clearly.

Discerning God's leading is a journey of faith, trust, and growth. As you quieten your mind and seek Him, He will make your paths straight. Trust in His goodness and timing, knowing that He desires to lead you into a fulfilling future. Hold on to Proverbs 3:5-6 as a reminder to lean on Him, and let His peace guide your heart.

The Importance of Patience: The Virtue of Patience in Waiting for God's Timing

Patience is a vital virtue, especially for singles seeking the right life partner. Psalm 27:14 reminds us, *"Wait for the Lord; be strong, and let your heart take courage; wait for the Lord!"* Waiting on God's timing means trusting in His perfect plan, even when the wait seems long or challenging. In this waiting period, God often uses the time to refine our character, deepen our relationship with Him, and prepare us for the future He has planned.

Benefits of Patience in Waiting

1. **Spiritual Growth:** Waiting allows us to grow closer to God and deepen our faith. It shifts our focus from impatience to trust.
2. **Preparation for Partnership:** God uses the waiting season to work on us, shaping us into the kind of partner He desires us to be.

3. **Avoiding Hasty Decisions:** Patience helps us discern wisely and avoid relationships that might not align with God's will.

Biblical Stories of Patience in Waiting

1. Isaac and Rebekah (Genesis 24)

Isaac waited patiently for the right partner, and God orchestrated a beautiful meeting through Abraham's servant. The servant prayed for specific signs to identify Isaac's future wife, and God answered, leading him to Rebekah. This story shows that God honors prayerful patience and provides in His time.

> ***Key Verse:*** *"Before he had finished praying, Rebekah came out with her jar on her shoulder." – Genesis 24:15*

2. Ruth and Boaz (Ruth 2-4)

Ruth's story is one of faithfulness, humility, and patience. After experiencing loss, Ruth focused on her responsibilities and remained loyal to her mother-in-law, Naomi. She met Boaz, a man of integrity, who recognised her character and became her husband. Their union was part of God's larger plan, as they became ancestors of King David and Jesus Christ.

> ***Key Verse:*** *"The Lord bless you, my daughter," Boaz replied. "This kindness is greater than that which you showed earlier: You have not run after the younger men, whether rich or poor." – Ruth 3:10*

3. Jacob and Rachel (Genesis 29)

Jacob loved Rachel deeply and worked for her father, Laban, for seven years to marry her. When Laban tricked him into marrying Leah first, Jacob worked an additional seven years for Rachel. Despite the delays and challenges, Jacob's patience and commitment were rewarded.

> ***Key Verse:*** *"So Jacob served seven years to get Rachel, but they seemed like only a few days to him because of his love for her." – Genesis 29:20*

Lessons for Singles from These Stories

1. **God's Timing is Perfect:** Trust that God is working behind the scenes to align events and people for His purpose in your life.
2. **Focus on Faithfulness:** While waiting, focus on serving God, growing spiritually, and developing your character.
3. **Prayerful Seeking:** Just as Abraham's servant prayed for guidance, seek God's direction earnestly in your journey.

Practical Steps to Cultivate Patience

1. **Meditate on Scripture:** Reflect on passages like Lamentations 3:25-26 – "The Lord is good to those who wait for him, to the soul who seeks him. It is good that one should wait quietly for the salvation of the Lord."

2. **Stay Active in God's Work:** Serve in your church or community, building relationships and skills that prepare you for a future partnership.
3. **Trust God's Promises:** Hold onto verses like

   Isaiah 40:31 – "But they who wait for the Lord shall renew their strength; they shall mount up with wings like eagles."

Modern-Day Stories of Waiting

1. Joyful Surrender: Sarah and John's Story

Sarah spent years praying for a life partner. Instead of becoming disheartened, she dedicated herself to mission work and personal growth. At a church retreat, she met John, whose values and purpose aligned with hers. They married a year later, thankful for the waiting season that prepared them for each other.

2. Trusting God's Timing: David and Angela's Journey

David struggled with impatience in his 30s, but after a season of prayer and mentoring, he learned to rest in God's timing. At a Bible study group, he met Angela, who had also been waiting patiently. Their shared faith and values laid the foundation for a strong marriage.

Encouragement for Singles

Patience is not about passivity but about trusting God actively. Waiting for the right partner in God's time ensures that you step into a relationship built on a strong spiritual foundation. Hold on to the promise of Psalm 27:14 and take courage, knowing that God's timing is always worth the wait.

6

Navigating The Dating Process

Dating, when approached with the right intentions, is a journey of discovery. This chapter provides practical tips on how to approach dating from a faith-based perspective, focusing on setting boundaries, identifying red flags, and fostering healthy communication.

Key Lessons:

Intentional Dating: Approach relationships with purpose, seeking to understand if the person is truly compatible with you for marriage.

Red Flags: Emotional manipulation, dishonesty, lack of respect, and unhealthy dependence are signs that a relationship may not be healthy.

Boundaries: Physical and emotional boundaries protect both individuals in a relationship and help them honour God in their actions.

Story Segment: Sarah's next relationship was different. She set boundaries early on, something she had failed to do in her previous relationships. Both she and her new boyfriend committed to prioritising spiritual growth and avoiding situations that would compromise their values.

Approaching Dating with Intention: The Importance of Setting Clear Intentions and Boundaries in Dating

Setting clear intentions and boundaries is essential to choosing the right partner and building a relationship that honours God. Clear intentions help establish mutual understanding, while healthy boundaries protect emotional, physical, and spiritual well-being. The Bible encourages wisdom, self-control, and purity in relationships, laying a foundation for a strong partnership.

Why Intentions and Boundaries Matter

Promotes Purposeful Dating:

Clear intentions ensure that both individuals are on the same page about the goals of the relationship. Amos 3:3 says, *"Do two walk together unless they have agreed to do so?"* Alignment of values and vision prevents confusion and frustration.

Protects Emotional and Spiritual Health:

Boundaries safeguard hearts and minds, reducing the likelihood of pain or regret. Proverbs 4:23 warns, *"Above all else, guard your heart, for everything you do flows from it."*

Fosters Respect and Growth:

Boundaries help partners respect each other's individuality and create space for healthy growth, fostering trust and stability.

Upholds Purity and Holiness:

God calls us to honour Him in our bodies and relationships. 1 Thessalonians 4:3-4 reminds us, "It is God's will that you should be sanctified: that you should avoid sexual immorality; that each of you should learn to control your own body in a way that is holy and honorable."

Examples of Healthy Boundaries in Dating

1. Physical Boundaries

Decide together what physical expressions of affection are appropriate, avoiding situations that lead to temptation.

Commit to honouring God with your body, as stated in 1 Corinthians 6:19-20: "Do you not know that your bodies are temples of the Holy Spirit... You are not your own; you were bought at a price."

Example: *A couple might agree to save kissing for later stages of the relationship or to avoid being alone in private spaces.*

2. Emotional Boundaries

Be mindful about how quickly you share deep personal struggles or emotions. Building emotional intimacy too quickly can create false perceptions of closeness.

Practice self-awareness and communicate your feelings clearly and respectfully.

Example: *Set a pace for how much personal information is shared early in the relationship, ensuring trust and commitment grow naturally.*

3. Spiritual Boundaries

Encourage each other's spiritual growth but maintain individual devotional practices. Avoid co-dependency in faith.

Guard against spiritual intimacy that mimics the depth of a marriage relationship.

> ***Example:*** *Pray together occasionally but avoid making spiritual practices like daily devotionals a primary bonding activity, as this can blur relational boundaries.*

4. Time Boundaries

Limit how much time you spend together to maintain balance in other areas of life, such as friendships, family, and personal goals.

Ensure that time spent is meaningful and not excessive to the point of neglecting other responsibilities.

> ***Example:*** *A couple might agree to meet a few times a week and set curfews to prevent overly long or late-night visits.*

5. Relational Boundaries

When it comes to relationships, boundaries are like the framework of a beautiful house. They provide structure, protect what's precious, and create a space where love can flourish. For anyone considering marriage, establishing healthy relational boundaries is essential. It's not about building walls to keep others out; rather, it's about setting up guardrails to guide a relationship toward mutual respect, trust, and growth.

Why Are Relational Boundaries Important?

Boundaries are a form of self-care. They help you define what you need and expect from a relationship while also, respecting the other person's individuality. Relational Boundaries play a vital role in:

Protecting Emotional Well-being

Emotional intimacy can be powerful but diving in too deeply or too quickly can sometimes lead to confusion or heartbreak. Boundaries help ensure that emotional connections grow at a healthy pace, fostering trust without overwhelming either person.

Clarifying Intentions

Clear boundaries communicate your values, expectations, and goals for the relationship. Whether it's about physical affection, how you spend time together, or even how you approach conflict, setting boundaries ensures both people are on the same page.

Cultivating Mutual Respect

A relationship where boundaries are respected sets the stage for mutual trust and understanding. It shows that both partners value each other's needs and are willing to honour them.

Preparing for Marriage

Marriage is about partnership, and good boundaries lay the groundwork for shared responsibilities, decision-making, and compromise. Learning how to set and maintain boundaries before marriage can make the transition smoother.

Key Areas to Consider for Relational Boundaries

Here are a few areas where setting boundaries can be especially helpful for singles preparing for marriage:

Emotional Boundaries

It's easy to overshare or rely too heavily on your partner for emotional support, especially early in the relationship. Take time to cultivate other supportive relationships, like with friends or family, to maintain balance.

Physical Boundaries

Physical intimacy is a deeply personal topic and one that requires open, honest communication. Decide together what feels right and respectful for your relationship, keeping your shared values and future goals in mind.

Time Boundaries

Spending time together is wonderful, but it's also important to maintain your individual interests, friendships, and routines. Healthy time boundaries can keep the relationship fresh and prevent burnout.

Financial Boundaries

Money can be a touchy subject, but it's wise to discuss financial habits and boundaries early. This could mean agreeing on who pays for what during dating or having conversations about future financial planning.

Spiritual Boundaries

If faith is an important part of your life, setting boundaries around spiritual practices and beliefs can help ensure alignment and mutual respect.

How to Establish Healthy Boundaries

Be Honest with Yourself

Reflect on your values, needs, and non-negotiables. The clearer you are about what matters to you, the easier it will be to communicate these to your partner.

Communicate Openly and Kindly

Boundaries aren't ultimatums. They're about expressing your needs in a way that invites collaboration. Use "I" statements, like "I feel more comfortable when we…" or "I need some time to think before making big decisions."

Stay Flexible

Relationships grow and change, so it's okay for boundaries to evolve over time. What matters is that both partners remain committed to open dialogue and mutual respect.

Enforce with Love

If a boundary is crossed, address it gently but firmly. Consistency shows that you value yourself and the relationship enough to uphold what you've agreed on.

Relational boundaries aren't about limiting love—they're about fostering it. They create a space where both partners can thrive as individuals while building something beautiful together. For single people preparing for marriage, investing in these boundaries now can lead to a stronger, healthier, and more joyful relationship down the road.

After all, the best marriages aren't just about finding the right person—they're about becoming the right partner.

And that journey begins with understanding, respecting, and honouring the boundaries that nurture love and respect.

Steps for Setting and Maintaining Boundaries

Pray for Wisdom:

Seek God's guidance in establishing boundaries and ask for strength to maintain them. James 1:5 encourages, *"If any of you lacks wisdom, you should ask God... and it will be given to you."*

Have Honest Conversations:

Discuss expectations and boundaries with your partner early in the relationship to foster mutual respect.

Write Them Down:

Documenting boundaries can help both parties stay accountable and revisit them when needed.

Seek Accountability:

Share your boundaries with a trusted mentor, pastor, or friend who can encourage and guide you.

Reassess Regularly:

As the relationship progresses, revisit boundaries to ensure they remain effective and relevant.

Biblical Examples of Boundaries

Joseph and Potiphar's Wife (Genesis 39:6-12):

Joseph fled from temptation, setting a firm boundary to maintain his integrity. His example teaches us to act decisively to avoid compromising situations.

Ruth and Boaz (Ruth 2-4):

Boaz upheld boundaries by ensuring Ruth's reputation was protected, demonstrating respect and honour.

Jesus' Relationships:

Jesus sets boundaries even in close relationships. He withdrew to pray alone (Luke 5:16) and maintained clarity about His mission, showing us the importance of prioritising God's will.

Encouragement for Singles

Boundaries are not restrictions; they are safeguarding that honour God and protect the beauty of a relationship. As you seek a partner, remember the words of Psalm 16:6: *"The boundary lines have fallen for me in pleasant places; surely I have a delightful inheritance."* Trust that boundaries, guided by God's wisdom, lead to blessings and fulfilment.

Spotting Red Flags and Warning Signs Before Marriage

When you're single and considering marriage, it's easy to focus on the excitement of building a life with someone. But amidst the butterflies and dreams, it's important to stay grounded and keep your eyes open for red flags and warning signs. These are the subtle (and sometimes glaring) indicators that a relationship might not be as healthy or God-honouring as it seems. Identifying them early can save you from heartbreak, disappointment, or even a marriage built on shaky ground.

Why Identifying Red Flags Early Is Important

Prevention Over Cure

Marriage is a lifelong commitment. It's far easier—and healthier—to address potential issues before walking down the aisle than to deal with them after you've made a covenant.

Avoiding Emotional Entanglements

The deeper you go emotionally, the harder it is to objectively assess a relationship. Recognising red flags early helps you make decisions with clarity rather than being clouded by attachment.

Obedience to God's Will

As believers, we're called to pursue relationships that honour God (2 Corinthians 6:14). Paying attention to warning signs helps ensure that your relationship aligns with biblical principles.

Protecting Your Future

Red flags often signal deeper issues that, if ignored, can lead to ongoing conflict, hurt, or even divorce. Early awareness allows you to seek counsel or, if necessary, walk away before committing to life.

Common Red Flags to Watch For

Lack of Respect

If your partner dismisses your opinions, belittles your ideas, or constantly puts their needs above yours, that's a serious concern. Respect is the foundation of a healthy relationship.

> ***Ephesians 5:33*** *instructs husbands to love their wives and wives to respect their husbands. Mutual respect is non-negotiable.*

Uncontrolled Anger

A partner who frequently loses their temper or handles disagreements with aggression may struggle with deeper emotional issues.

> ***Proverbs 22:24–25*** *warns against associating with a hot-tempered person, as their behaviour can lead to trouble.*

Dishonesty

Trust is crucial in any relationship. If your partner lies, hides things, or evades accountability, take it as a serious warning.

> ***Proverbs 12:22*** *says, "The Lord detests lying lips, but he delights in people who are trustworthy."*

Controlling Behaviour

If your partner tries to dictate what you wear, who you see, or how you spend your time, it's a sign of insecurity and a lack of trust.

> ***1 Corinthians 13:4–5*** *reminds us that love does not envy, is not proud, and does not dishonour others. True love allows freedom and respect.*

Spiritual Mismatch

If you're a believer and your partner isn't, it can lead to significant challenges in building a shared vision for your life.

> ***2 Corinthians 6:14*** *cautions against being "unequally yoked with unbelievers." Shared faith is foundational for a God-centred marriage.*

Neglect of Responsibilities

A partner who consistently shirks responsibilities—whether financial, emotional, or relational—may not be ready for the commitment of marriage.

> ***1 Timothy 5:8*** *states that providing for one's family is a sign of integrity and faith.*

Addictive Behaviours

Struggles with substance abuse, pornography, or other addictions can deeply impact a relationship. While change is possible, it requires willingness and accountability.

Isolation

If your partner discourages your relationships with family and friends or insists that you depend solely on them, it's a major red flag. Healthy love welcomes the community.

> ***Proverbs 11:14*** *emphasises the importance of seeking counsel and having a supportive community.*

How to Respond When You Notice Red Flags

Pray for Discernment

Ask God for wisdom and clarity to see the situation as it truly is. James 1:5 promises that God will give wisdom to those who ask.

Seek Godly Counsel

Talk to trusted mentors, pastors, or friends who can provide objective insights. *Proverbs 15:22 says, "Plans fail for lack of counsel, but with many advisers, they succeed."*

Have Honest Conversations

Address the red flag directly with your partner. Sometimes, they may not even realise their behaviour is problematic. Healthy relationships thrive on open communication.

Don't Ignore Your Gut

If something feels off, take it seriously. Often, the Holy Spirit nudges us through unease to protect us from harm.

Be Willing to Walk Away

If the red flags persist and efforts to resolve them are unsuccessful, it may be best to end the relationship. Walking away now can save you from deeper pain later.

Marriage is a beautiful, God-ordained union, but it's not one to rush into blindly. By keeping your eyes open to red flags and seeking God's guidance, you can enter this sacred covenant with confidence and peace. Remember, the right relationship will reflect God's love, patience, and grace—and will allow you to grow into the person He has called you to be.

After all, it's better to wait for the right person in God's timing than to settle for less and regret it later. Trust Him to guide your heart and your steps.

Checklist for Evaluating a Potential Partner

Use the following checklist to prayerfully assess whether a potential partner aligns with God's standards and your values.

Character Evaluation

Are they honest and trustworthy? Look for consistency in words and actions.

> ***Proverbs 10:9:*** *"Whoever walks in integrity walks securely."*

Do they show kindness and patience? Evaluate how they treat others, especially in challenging situations.

> ***Colossians 3:12:*** *"Clothe yourselves with compassion, kindness, humility, gentleness, and patience."*

Are they respectful of boundaries? Ensure they honour your physical, emotional, and spiritual limits.

> ***1 Corinthians 13:5:*** *"Love... is not rude, it is not self-seeking."*

Spiritual Compatibility

Do they share your faith and values? A shared faith foundation strengthens long-term compatibility.

> ***Amos 3:3:*** *"Do two walk together unless they have agreed to do so?"*

Are they committed to spiritual growth? Look for a desire to grow in Christ and encourage your spiritual journey.

> ***Matthew 6:33:*** *"Seek first his kingdom and his righteousness."*

Relational Dynamics

Do they communicate openly and respectfully? Healthy relationships are marked by honest, respectful dialogue.

> ***Proverbs 15:1:*** *"A gentle answer turns away wrath, but a harsh word stirs up anger."*

Do they support your goals and dreams? A supportive partner will encourage you to pursue your God-given purpose.

> ***Proverbs 27:17:*** *"As iron sharpens iron, so one person sharpens another."*

Conflict Resolution

How do they handle disagreements? Observe if they resolve conflicts calmly or resort to anger and blame.

> *Ephesians 4:26: "In your anger do not sin."*

Are they forgiving and gracious? Look for a willingness to forgive rather than hold grudges.

> *Colossians 3:13: "Bear with each other and forgive one another."*

Choosing the right partner requires discernment, prayer, and trust in God's guidance. Regularly evaluate potential relationships through the lens of Scripture and seek wise counsel when needed. Remember Proverbs 4:23: *"Above all else, guard your heart, for everything you do flows from it."* By being intentional and grounded in biblical principles, you can build a relationship that reflects God's love and glorifies Him.

Fostering Healthy Communication: The Importance of Healthy Communication While Dating

Communication is the foundation of any strong relationship, and it's especially vital during dating. Healthy communication fosters understanding, builds trust, and creates a safe space for expressing feelings, expectations, and concerns. For singles, mastering communication skills during dating helps lay a foundation for a God-honouring partnership.

The Bible emphasises the power of words in relationships. Proverbs 18:21 states, *"The tongue has the power of life and death, and those who love it will eat its fruit."* Speaking truthfully and lovingly can strengthen connections, while poor communication can harm relationships.

Why Healthy Communication Matters

1. **Builds Trust:** Open and honest communication demonstrates integrity and fosters trust.
2. **Resolves Conflicts:** Addressing issues early prevents misunderstandings from growing.
3. **Encourages Emotional Intimacy:** Sharing feelings and thoughts deepens understanding.
4. **Honors God:** Speaking with love, respect, and truthfulness reflects biblical principles. Ephesians 4:29: "Do not let any unwholesome talk

come out of your mouths, but only what is helpful for building others up according to their needs."

Tips for Effective Communication in Dating

1. Speak Truth in Love

- Express your thoughts and feelings clearly and kindly.
- Avoid passive-aggressiveness or harsh words.

Ephesians 4:15: "Speak the truth in love."

2. Listen Actively

- Pay attention without interrupting.
- Show empathy by summarising what the other person said.
- Ask clarifying questions to ensure understanding.

3. Use "I" Statements

- Frame concerns from your perspective to avoid blame.
- Focus on how you feel rather than what the other person did.

4. Be Honest and Vulnerable

- Share your feelings and expectations openly.
- Avoid hiding your true thoughts out of fear of rejection.

5. Practice Patience and Grace

- Allow room for misunderstandings and growth.
- Respond with kindness, even when conversations are difficult.
- Colossians 4:6: "Let your conversation be always full of grace, seasoned with salt."

Effective communication is a skill that grows with practice and prayer. Approach conversations with humility and a willingness to learn. Trust in God's wisdom to guide your words, as Proverbs 3:5-6 reminds us: *"Trust in the Lord with all your heart and lean not on your own understanding; in all your ways submit to him, and he will make your paths straight."* By communicating in a way that honours God, you can build relationships that are honest, loving, and enduring.

7

Trusting God with the Outcome:

Making the most of the Waiting Season

The season of waiting for marriage can sometimes feel like an endless pause, especially when the desire for a partner is strong. But rather than viewing this time as a delay, it's helpful to see it as a divine appointment—a season God uses to prepare, refine, and bless you. The waiting period isn't about just sitting idly; it's about active growth, purpose, and trusting God's timing.

The waiting process can feel unbearable, and doubt can creep in. This chapter will encourage you to trust God with your future, even when the path ahead seems unclear. God's plan is perfect, even when it doesn't match our desires.

Story Segment: After ending her relationship, Sarah spent a long season single, feeling like she had missed out on love. She wrestled with God in prayer, asking why things weren't working out for her. Slowly, she began to trust that God's timing was different from her own. She found contentment in her single season, investing in her spiritual growth, friendships, and passions.

Why the Waiting Season Matters

Spiritual Preparation

Marriage is a beautiful but challenging covenant that requires spiritual maturity. The waiting season is a time for you to deepen your relationship with God, building a foundation that will strengthen your future marriage.

Character Development

God often uses waiting to mold us into the person He wants us to be. This is a time to work on patience, selflessness, and humility—qualities essential for a successful marriage.

Fulfilling God's Purpose Now

Your life's purpose doesn't begin when you get married. God has specific plans for you in this season. Discovering and walking in them ensures your life is rich and meaningful, whether single or married.

Avoiding Impatience and Settling

Rushing into the wrong relationship out of impatience can lead to heartbreak. The waiting period helps you discern God's best for your life.

What to Do While Waiting

Here are some practical steps to make the most of your season of singleness, along with Biblical wisdom to guide you:

1. Grow Closer to God

Use this time to cultivate a deeper relationship with God. Marriage is designed to reflect God's love for His people (Ephesians 5:25–27), so knowing Him intimately now will prepare you to love your future spouse well.

Practical Steps:

- Spend time daily in prayer and Bible study.
- Serve in your church or community.
- Listen for God's voice about His plans for your life.

Matthew 6:33: "Seek first his kingdom and his righteousness, and all these things will be given to you as well."

2. Develop Yourself

Marriage doesn't complete you; God does (Colossians 2:10). Use this time to grow into the person God created you to be.

Practical Steps:

- Pursue your passions, education, or career.
- Work on emotional health by addressing unresolved hurts or insecurities.
- Learn practical skills that can enrich your future marriage, such as managing finances or cooking.

Colossians 3:23: "Whatever you do, work at it with all your heart, as working for the Lord, not for human masters."

3. Build Strong Relationships

The waiting season is an opportunity to nurture meaningful connections with family, friends, and mentors. A healthy support system will not only enrich your current life but also strengthen you in marriage.

Practical Steps:

- Spend time investing in your friendships.
- Surround yourself with godly mentors who can provide guidance.
- Be an encouragement to others who are also waiting.

Ecclesiastes 4:9:"Two are better than one, because they have a good return for their labor."

4. Prepare for Marriage, But Don't Obsess Over It

There's wisdom in preparing for marriage, but it shouldn't consume your thoughts or identity. Let your focus remain on God and His plans for you now.

Practical Steps:

- Read books or attend seminars on building healthy relationships.
- Reflect on the qualities you want in a spouse and the qualities you want to bring to a marriage.
- Pray for your future spouse, asking God to prepare their heart as well.

Philippians 4:6: "Do not be anxious about anything, but in every situation, by prayer and petition, with thanksgiving, present your requests to God."

5. Trust God's Timing

The waiting season can be frustrating, but it's important to trust that God knows what's best for you and when. His plans are always better than anything we could imagine.

Practical Steps:

- Remind yourself of God's faithfulness through past seasons.
- Focus on gratitude for the present.
- Resist comparing your journey to others.

Ecclesiastes 3:1: "There is a time for everything, and a season for every activity under the heavens."

Psalm 27:14: "Wait for the Lord; be strong and take heart and wait for the Lord."

6. Serve Others

One of the most fulfilling ways to use your time is by serving others. It shifts your focus from waiting to giving, and it reflects God's love in action.

Practical Steps:

- Volunteer in ministries or charities that align with your passions.
- Be a mentor to younger believers or a support to those in need.
- Use your gifts to glorify God in tangible ways.

Matthew 23:11: "The greatest among you will be your servant."

1 Peter 4:10: "Each of you should use whatever gift you have received to serve others, as faithful stewards of God's grace."

The waiting season is not a punishment—it's preparation. It's a time for you to grow, thrive, and experience God's goodness in unique ways. By using this season wisely, you're not only preparing for marriage but also deepening your relationship with God and discovering the fullness of life He has for you.

Remember, God is never late. Trust His perfect timing, knowing that He is working all things together for your good (Romans 8:28). And when the time comes, you'll step into marriage not just as someone who waited, but as someone who prepared with faith, and purpose, and joy.

8

Building A Christ-Centred Relationship:

Preparing to Choose the Right Partner for Marriage: A Detailed Guide for Singles

Choosing the right partner to marry is one of the most significant and life-altering decisions you will ever make. It requires wisdom, patience, and intentionality. Marriage is a covenant relationship designed by God, and choosing a partner is not merely about compatibility but about finding someone with whom you can fulfil God's purpose for your life.

Trust that God has a plan for your life, and His timing is always perfect. When the right person comes into your life, you will be ready—not just because you waited, but because you prepared your heart, mind, and spirit for the journey of marriage.

When the right partner comes, the work doesn't stop. This chapter explores how to build a relationship rooted in Christ and designed to glorify God.

Story Segment: Sarah eventually met Jacob, a man whose character, faith, and love for God aligned with her values. Their relationship wasn't perfect but built on prayer, accountability, and a shared mission to serve others. They prayed, studied scripture, and sought guidance from their church community.

The Principles for Building a Relationship Rooted in Christ

This guide will provide detailed advice to help singles prepare themselves to choose wisely, drawing from practical insights and Biblical principles.

1. Look for Godly Character, Not Just Chemistry

Physical attraction and emotional chemistry are important, but they are not enough to sustain a lifelong relationship. Focus on the potential partner's character, values, and relationship with God.

Qualities to Look For:

Spiritual Maturity: A partner who genuinely loves God and seeks to live according to His Word.

Kindness and Respect: Someone who treats you and others with patience, compassion, and honour.

Integrity: A person whose actions align with their words and who demonstrates honesty and trustworthiness.

Proverbs 31:30: "Charm is deceptive, and beauty is fleeting; but a woman who fears the Lord is to be praised."

Galatians 5:22–23: "The fruit of the Spirit is love, joy, peace, forbearance, kindness, goodness, faithfulness, gentleness, and self-control."

2. Observe How They Handle Relationships

A person's interactions with others can reveal a lot about their character and potential as a spouse. How they treat their family, friends, and even strangers are a window into their values and behaviour.

Practical Observations:

Family Dynamics: Do they honour their parents and maintain healthy relationships with their siblings?

Friendships: Are they surrounded by supportive, godly friends who hold them accountable?

Conflict Resolution: How do they handle disagreements or stressful situations? Do they respond with grace or aggression?

> *Luke 6:31: "Do to others as you would have them do to you."*

3. Be Patient and Trust God's Timing

Impatience can lead to settling for less than God's best. Trust that God's timing is perfect, and He knows what you need and when you need it.

Practical Steps:

Focus on the Present: Invest in personal growth and pursue your current passions and callings.

Avoid Comparison: Resist the temptation to measure your journey against others who may already be married.

Pray for Your Future Spouse: Commit them to God and ask Him to prepare both of your hearts.

> *Ecclesiastes 3:1: "There is a time for everything, and a season for every activity under the heavens."*

> *Lamentations 3:25: "The Lord is good to those whose hope is in him, to the one who seeks him."*

4. Seek Wisdom and Counsel

God often uses others to guide us. Trusted mentors, family, and spiritual leaders can provide valuable insights and help you make a wise decision.

Practical Steps:

Involve Trusted Mentors: Share your thoughts about your relationship with someone who knows you well and can offer godly advice.

Be Open to Feedback: Listen to constructive criticism and consider it prayerfully.

Surround Yourself with Prayer: Ask your mentors, family, and friends to pray for discernment on your behalf.

> *Proverbs 15:22: "Plans fail for lack of counsel, but with many advisers they succeed."*

5. Evaluate Compatibility

Marriage requires alignment in key areas such as faith, life goals, and communication. Practical compatibility can make a significant difference in the success of your relationship.

Areas to Consider:

Spiritual Alignment: Do you both prioritise God and share a commitment to serving Him?

Life Goals: Are your dreams and aspirations complementary, or do they clash?

Conflict Resolution: Can you communicate effectively and resolve disagreements healthily?

> *Amos 3:3: "Can two walk together unless they are agreed?"*

6. Pray Without Ceasing

Prayer is your most powerful tool in preparing to choose the right partner. Consistently seeking God's guidance ensures that you're aligned with His will for your life.

Practical Steps:

Pray for Clarity: Ask God to reveal any red flags or affirmations about the relationship.

Surrender Your Desires: Trust God's plan, even if it differs from your expectations.

Pray for Confirmation: Seek peace and assurance from the Holy Spirit.

> *Thessalonians 5:17–18: "Pray continually, give thanks in all circumstances; for this is God's will for you in Christ Jesus."*

A Journey of Faith and Love

This reflects on the journey, reminding singles that choosing the right partner is not about finding the "perfect" person but finding the person God has chosen for you. Trusting God's timing, preparing your heart, and seeking His will are key to finding a partner who will walk with you in faith and love.

> **Story Segment**: Sarah and Jacob eventually married, and their union was a testament to God's faithfulness. Their story reminds readers that

though the path to finding the right partner may be filled with struggles and lessons, trusting in God's guidance leads to a relationship that reflects His love and purpose.

Foundation of Faith:

Establishing a relationship rooted in Christ is a transformative journey that singles can embark on by first nurturing their personal relationship with God. Colossians 3:14 emphasises the importance of love, stating, "And over all these virtues put on love, which binds them all together in perfect unity." For singles seeking to build a relationship that honours Christ, it is essential to be intentional about spiritual growth, emotional readiness, and a deep understanding of what it means to love with God's love. Here are practical steps for preparing oneself and integrating faith into a future Christ-centred relationship:

1. Praying:

Develop Spiritual Disciplines: Strengthening your relationship with God through daily prayer, Bible study, and worship will equip you with the spiritual tools needed to lead a Christ-centred life. A strong personal relationship with God is foundational, as it helps cultivate the kind of love, patience, and kindness that will be needed in any relationship.

Seek Spiritual Mentorship: Having a mentor who shares your values can help guide you in the process of preparing for a Christ-centred relationship. They can provide wisdom and accountability in navigating the challenges of singleness and dating.

2. Cultivate Christlike Character

Embrace the Fruit of the Spirit: Galatians 5:22-23 outlines the qualities of the Holy Spirit, such as love, joy, peace, patience, kindness, goodness, faithfulness, gentleness, and self-control. As a single person, focusing on these qualities can help you become the type of person who is ready to love and serve others, especially in a relationship.

Work on Emotional Health: Emotional maturity is essential when preparing for a relationship. Take time to understand your emotions, heal from past hurts, and address any unresolved issues. Practising forgiveness and embracing grace will enable you to bring a healthier version of yourself to a future relationship.

3. Set Clear, God-Honouring Standards

Know Your Boundaries: Understanding your values, boundaries, and what you're looking for in a partner is crucial. This helps you avoid settling for someone who does not share your faith or has incompatible life goals. A Christ-centred relationship should align with biblical values of mutual respect, love, and commitment.

Seek a Partner Who Shares Your Faith: 2 Corinthians 6:14 encourages believers not to be unequally yoked with unbelievers. When entering into a relationship, it's vital to find someone who shares your love for Christ and values the same principles. This foundation will allow both individuals to support and encourage each other's spiritual growth.

4. Practice Patience and Trust in God's Timing

Trust God's Timing: Building a Christ-centred relationship doesn't need to be rushed. God's timing is perfect and trusting Him will allow you to wait for the right person at the right time. In moments of impatience, pray for contentment and faith that God will provide.

Prepare for Marriage, Not Just Dating: Dating should be viewed as a step toward marriage, and as you prepare for a relationship, consider how your actions and decisions will reflect a future commitment. If marriage is your goal, pursue it with intentionality and focus on becoming the person you hope to marry.

5. Integrate Faith into the Relationship

Pray Together: One of the most powerful ways to integrate faith into a relationship is through prayer. Regularly praying together fosters intimacy, helps both partners grow spiritually, and strengthens the bond. Make prayer a priority in every stage of the relationship.

Engage in Bible Study: Incorporating Bible study into the relationship not only strengthens your personal relationship with God but also builds a strong spiritual foundation as a couple. Whether through individual studies or couples' devotionals, learning and growing in God's Word together is essential.

Serve Together: Look for opportunities to serve God together. Whether it's volunteering at church, participating in a mission trip, or helping those in need, serving together creates a shared sense of purpose and allows both partners to grow in their faith while making a positive impact on others.

Communicate with Love and Respect: A Christ-centred relationship involves healthy, open communication. Ephesians 4:15 encourages speaking the truth in love, which helps build trust and transparency. Use your words to uplift and encourage each other, always seeking to reflect the love of Christ.

6. Stay Committed to Growth and Accountability

Accountability Partners: It's helpful to have individuals in your life who will hold you accountable to your values and commitments. Whether it's a mentor, a close friend, or a pastor, accountability ensures you stay on track in your walk with Christ and your pursuit of a godly relationship.

Seek Continuous Growth: Never stop growing in your relationship with God or in your personal development. A healthy relationship is built on two individuals who are committed to ongoing spiritual, emotional, and personal growth. By continually striving to improve and seeking God's guidance, you'll be better prepared for a relationship that reflects His love.

A relationship rooted in Christ seeks to honour God first and foremost. Singles can prepare themselves for this type of relationship by Prioritising their relationship with God, cultivating Christlike character, setting God-honouring standards, and practicing patience. Once in a relationship, the key is to integrate faith by praying together, studying

Scripture, serving God, and maintaining open communication built on love and respect. By doing so, you establish a foundation of love that reflects the unity and selflessness described in Colossians 3:14. Ultimately, by allowing God to lead the way, a Christ-centred relationship will flourish with grace, purpose, and lasting love.

A Word Of Encouragement

In a world where relationships can often feel rushed or pressured, singles need to embrace hope, trust in God's perfect timing, and stay steadfast in their faith. The journey of waiting for the right partner can sometimes be filled with doubt or impatience, but God's promises and plans for your life are always filled with hope, purpose, and love. As you navigate the season of singleness, remember that your value is not in a relationship but in your identity in Christ. By trusting God's perfect plan and remaining faithful, you will experience the peace that comes from knowing He has a beautiful future laid out for you.

1. Embrace the Hope of God's Promises

The Bible is full of promises that offer hope to singles, reassuring them that God's plan is good, His timing is perfect, and His provision is faithful. Jeremiah 29:11 reminds us: *"For I know the plans I have for you, declares the Lord, plans for welfare and not for evil, to give you a future and a hope."*

This promise is not just for the married or those in relationships but for everyone—singles included. In the waiting season, we can trust that God's plan includes our relational needs and desires, even if they are not fulfilled on our timeline. Hope is built on the assurance that God's plan for us is full of purpose and love, even as we wait.

2. Trust in God's Timing

One of the most significant challenges for singles is understanding and accepting God's timing. It can be difficult to remain hopeful when the desire for a partner feels overwhelming, especially if the wait seems long.

However, Romans 8:25 reminds us: *"But if we hope for what we do not see, we wait for it with patience."*

Patience is key in this season. Trusting that God's timing is always perfect and that He sees the bigger picture allows us to embrace the process rather than rush through it. God's timing isn't just about when the partner will arrive; it's about preparing us, molding us, and positioning us to meet someone who will be the right fit according to His will.

3. Focus on Personal Growth and Purpose

Rather than focusing solely on the absence of a partner, singles can find hope and fulfilment in personal growth and pursuing God's purpose. This is a season to focus on becoming the best version of yourself—spiritually, emotionally, and physically. As you draw nearer to God and grow in your relationship with Him, you become more prepared for the partner He has destined for you.

In 1 Corinthians 7:34, Paul encourages believers to focus on devotion to God during singleness: *"An unmarried woman is concerned about the Lord's affairs: Her aim is to be devoted to the Lord in both body and spirit."*

Use this time to deepen your relationship with God, to serve others, and to be faithful in the work He has entrusted to you. As you faithfully pursue His purpose for your life, you align yourself with His plan, which is often greater than anything you could have imagined on your own.

4. Know that God Sees Your Desires

God created the desire for companionship, and He knows your heart. Psalm 37:4 encourages us to: *"Delight yourself in the Lord, and He will give you the desires of your heart."*

While it may feel like your desires are unmet, God is not indifferent to them. He sees your longing for a relationship, your desire for companionship, and your wish to build a life with someone. The key is to trust that God will fulfill these desires in His perfect way and at the right time. As you remain faithful to Him, you can trust that He will either provide the partner you desire or guide you toward a fulfilling life as you wait for His best.

5. Learn to Trust and Wait in Faith

Hope in God's plan requires faith. Faith that He is working even when we can't see it, faith that He is preparing both us and the right partner for the future. Proverbs 3:5-6 reminds us to: *"Trust in the Lord with all your heart, and lean not on your own understanding; in all your ways submit to Him, and He will make your paths straight."*

When you trust in God's perfect plan, you can have peace in the waiting. Instead of anxiously looking for love or forcing relationships, trust that God knows what is best for you and is working things out behind the scenes. Waiting in faith allows you to rest in the certainty that God will not leave you disappointed.

6. Lean on God's Faithfulness and Love

The journey of singleness can sometimes feel lonely, but God's faithfulness remains constant. Isaiah 40:31 says: "But those who hope in the Lord will renew their strength. They will soar on wings like eagles; they will run and not grow weary, they will walk and not be faint."

As you hope in the Lord, your strength is renewed. You are not walking alone; God is with you every step of the way. He is your refuge and your strength, the one who sustains you during the seasons of waiting. Lean into His love and allow His presence to fill the spaces that sometimes feel empty.

7. Trust that God Knows What You Need

Finally, remember that God knows what you need even before you ask (Matthew 6:8). While we may have an ideal vision of the partner we want, God knows the person who will truly complement you, encourage you in your faith, and challenge you to grow. The person He leads you to will be the one who will walk alongside you in God's purpose for your life, not just as a romantic partner but as a spiritual companion. Trust that His choices are always for your good.

Hope for the Future

The journey of waiting is one of preparation and trust. The hope we have in Christ is not a fleeting hope; it is rooted in the truth that God's love for us is steadfast, and He is faithful to fulfil His promises. While waiting for a partner may sometimes feel challenging, it is an opportunity to grow closer to God, to serve others, and to prepare for the future He has planned. Remain steadfast in your faith, trusting that God is working in His perfect timing, and in His perfect way, He will provide the right person for you.

Ultimately, our hope is not in the desire for a partner but in the unshakable faith that God's plans for us are filled with hope, purpose, and an abundance of His love. Keep trusting, keep hoping, and keep waiting, for God's perfect plan is worth the wait.

Printed in Great Britain
by Amazon

63133844R00139